The big picture
for small churches
—and large ones, too!

How to thrive and survive as a small congregation

John Benton

EP BOOKS

Registered Office: 140 Coniscliffe Road, Darlington, Co. Durham, UK DL3 7RT

www.epbooks.org
admin@epbooks.org

EP Books are distributed in the USA by:

www.jplbooks.com
orders@jplbooks.com

and

100fThose Ltd
www.100ofthose.com
sales.us@100ofthose.com

First published 2005

Second impression 2010

This edition 2020

British Library Cataloguing in Publication Data available

ISBN: 978-1-78397-302-6

To the Lord's
faithful and often despised
little flocks
all over the world

Contents

Contents

Preface to the 2020 edition

When I wrote this book over 15 years ago, I had quite a battle with the then editor—who I hasten to say is a good guy—to get the words 'Small Churches' into the title. He felt the very words might discourage people from buying it. We all tend to be more immediately attracted to things which come across as uplifting and successful.

Since then there has been a growing recognition of the need to come alongside, support and revitalise smaller churches and many good people and Christian organisations have turned their minds to this great challenge.

There are a number of causes for encouragement as I survey the scene.

First, I am thrilled to see that some Bible colleges and training schemes have begun to specifically address the needs of little congregations in their courses. In fact sometime ago I actually took a phone call from a seminary professor from the Netherlands asking me how he could get hold of more copies of this book because it dealt with just the topics he felt were most relevant to those training for the ministry in his country.

Second, it is wonderful to see a number of younger men starting out in the ministry who have been prepared to jump in at the deep end and commit themselves and their families to rebuilding churches which have dwindled. One of these wrote this:

> In the summer of 2013 I was encouraged by one godly retired pastor to preach at a small church in southwest London. In spite of the church having been without a pastor for a number of years, I rather naively thought little of the summer visit. However, when my wife and I met the very small faithful group of Christians gathering there we instantly felt an affinity. The church, which fitted none of my aforementioned ministerial ideals, called me to be their pastor.

That young man and his family have gone to the church and got involved with a passion. The church has begun to change and now there is real hope for the future.

Third, I am encouraged to say that God himself is in the work of revitalizing smaller congregations. One particular story sticks out. The church had actually closed. But one man of faith I know felt under God that he should seek to open it again. On Easter Sunday a few years ago the church had a service, many well-wishers came, and the man preached. But the following Sunday of course reality kicked in. He went to the building, opened it up and besides himself nobody came. What was he to do. He prayed and decided that whether or not there was a congregation he would have a service. So on his own he sang, read the Scriptures, prayed and preached. The service came to an end. He put on his coat and went outside and began locking up. Just then an African woman came up to him. 'What have you being doing?' she asked. 'I've been praising God,' replied my friend. 'But you were on your own,' she said. 'Yes, I know' he confessed. 'Well,' she said, 'if you have a service next week, I will come.' It turned out that the lady was fairly new to the UK, she had seen the empty church building near her home, and had been praying that the Lord would do something. Over the next few months, first one and then others, began to come along. The church now numbers around fifty worshippers on Sundays and has its own pastor again. God it seems is not just in the business of church revitalization, but of church resurrection!

And if God is concerned to help small churches, it must be a good thing for us to get involved with too.

John Benton,
Guildford, March 2020

Introduction

A few years ago I was asked to go and give two papers to a conference of pastors, elders and deacons in the north of England on the subject of encouraging small churches. As I prayed and studied for that occasion, I began to feel very burdened for the many little flocks up and down the land. I felt touched by their struggles.

So often they are not only sneered at by the world, but sometimes feel belittled as the poor relations by Christians who have the benefit of enjoying the life of a larger fellowship. This book is something I have felt driven to write, hopefully as an expression of the Lord's love to churches which may feel weak and in need.

What is a small church? How do you define small? There are a couple of issues here.

Firstly, do you define the size of a church by its paper membership, or by the attendance at its meetings, particularly on Sundays? I have tended to think in terms of regular attendance and commitment. This is the only sensible way of looking at how big a church is for practical and gospel purposes.

Secondly, given that way of assessing things, how do we decide the boundaries between small, average and larger churches? In answering this question I spoke briefly with an organization that produces a lot of statistics about churches. Their rule of thumb went something like this. Churches with a usual attendance of over 300 people were looked upon as very large. More than 150 people put the church in the 'large' bracket. Over 50 or 60 people meant you belonged to the 'average' category. But less than 50 or 60 people meant that they looked upon the church as small.

Obviously all this is somewhat arbitrary and subjective. I am sure there are many little congregations, perhaps in rural settings, where if they saw as many as 50 people in the congregation on Sunday morning they would think revival had broken out. Nevertheless, it is churches with less than 50 people committed to them that I have in mind. And I suppose my heart is with groups which are even smaller than that.

The church where I serve is a good church and the people have been very good to me over the years. We started just in the 'small' category and now there are more of us. We have been blessed as we have tried to work out in just a little way some of the ideas discussed in this book. However, we are far from perfect and I cannot say that we are an exact example of all that I advocate in this book. We are all sinners and do not always measure up to all we would like to be.

However, having said that, hopefully, the contents of this book will be a help and encouragement to all churches, small and large. Many of the issues we explore are relevant to every church no matter how many people attend. Satan attacks churches regardless of size. We need to be clear on the gospel whether we are few or many. We must all access the resources of the Holy Spirit's power, for 'the arm of the flesh will fail', however many we are. The qualities of a healthy church are the same no matter how big or little we may be.

I have to acknowledge my indebtedness to Stuart Olyott, who in one brief conversation gave me some very helpful ideas about the way forward for small churches. I have tried to write this book for both church members and church leaders. So, whatever part you play in the body of Christ, and whatever church you are from, may the Lord use these pages to give new vision and enthusiasm. The Lord Jesus has promised, 'I will build my church.'

1.
The choice for small churches

If you are part of a small church you have a choice. You can choose either to look upon the small size of the congregation as a reason to be discouraged and downhearted; or you can choose to see the church's smallness as a reason why you might be in just the church God can use.

Where am I coming from with that last statement? Is it just foolish optimism? I don't think it is. Here is my reasoning.

God's thoughts are not our thoughts. He does not do things the way the world expects. One might say, with reverence, that our Father is often rather a 'lateral' thinker. Our God is a God who uses the lowly and despised to shame the big and glamorous, and selects the weak things to shame the strong, that all the glory might go to him (1 Corinthians 1:27). Is your church small and weak? Then you might well be in just the right condition to bring most glory to God.

Think about it for a moment. Who receives the glory when someone makes a profession of faith in Christ? No one these days is surprised if someone 'gets religion' at a large meeting with masses of techno-hype, heaps of emotional music and a handsome preacher renowned for his theatricality. 'That's the kind of thing that happens in crowds,' people say. They simply put it down to hysteria, or the need to belong, or the kind of psychological manipulation that can occur, consciously or unconsciously, when people gather in big numbers.

But if people are truly converted to Christ in a little chapel attended by two old ladies, a blind man and his dog, people will ask real questions! 'What on earth is going on here?' 'I can't see the attraction!' 'What could have possibly got into them?' Non-Christian relatives and friends might just be astonished. They could well see such conversions as the miracle that they truly are. The glory goes to God.

Who's counting?

It was with this philosophy about the potential usefulness of smaller churches that I entered the Christian ministry. I was a young man who had never been able to study full-time at a Bible college. (How I wish now that I had!) But I had begun to preach a little. Then, one August I was asked to go and preach at a church in the south of England. It was a day never to be forgotten for my wife and I. The congregation I preached to that day was to become the church to which God would send us. The building was unremarkable, and the people were lovely ordinary folk. I remember that the sermon I preached that morning was from 2 Samuel 24 on the foolishness of David's numbering of Israel's fighting men. How we love to think that strength is in numbers, when God says that it is 'not by might nor by power, but by my Spirit' (Zechariah 4:6). My message was straightforward. It was nothing to write home about. But somehow at the end of that day as Ann and I drove home, we knew deep in our hearts that God was calling us to that place and those people. We looked at each other in the car, and with a mixture of trepidation and elation we knew that it was there that our future would be.

It was not a very big church. The congregation was around 50 to 60, I suppose; I do not really know. Having preached on David's mistake of head counting, I vowed I would never do it. But what I did know was that there were other very big churches in the town with hundreds of people in the congregations. Somehow, I came to suspect that our little church was looked down upon by the bigger churches. We were despised. We were old-fashioned. It could have been a wrong perception on my part; I do not wish to lay any blame. But that was how it seemed.

Eventually, after more visits to the church, just as God had intimated on that first day, the call to the pastorate came. As someone with no previous experience, taking on the church was quite a daunting task. I do not think I would have survived except for the faithful group of elders around me. But in particular, the question of fostering a positive attitude and having faith that God could bless the church, when many people in the town gave the impression that they thought that over the years God had passed our congregation by and blessed others, was a real challenge.

Then the truth dawned on me. God is the God who derives most glory from situations that other people have written off. The depth of the darkness makes the starlight even more wonderful. The impossibility of a set of circumstances can be used by God to show his splendour. He is the God of little David versus mighty Goliath. He is the God of Ezekiel's vision. The valley of dry bones can become a mighty army. Most significantly, though Jesus was dead and buried, God is the God who loves to raise the dead to life. He is the God who brings the light of Easter morning out of the midnight of Good Friday. As these Scripture truths bore in upon me in the early years of the ministry, faith and hope that God could and would work in and through the church was kindled and maintained. To his praise, over time, the church has grown, and another church has been planted (or replanted) as well. God uses churches that others have written off. I hope that encourages you as it encourages me.

Small beginnings

We live in a society that worships at the shrine of size. We buy our food at 'supermarkets' and 'hyper-markets'. 'Monster' music events are promoted for the young. 'Mega' sales are advertised in department stores. 'Blockbuster' movies appear at our cinemas. In the world's eyes, if something is not big, it does not deserve attention. It is not easy to be upbeat about a church with just a few in the congregation when we live alongside such a cultural bias. But we are called to walk by faith and not by sight.

Perhaps when you saw the title of this opening chapter you thought that the choice discussed here for the small church would concern whether or not to close down. But that is not the agenda we will consider in this book. God can and does use small churches. It is good not only to ponder the teaching of Scripture concerning his use of small things, but it is also helpful to scan church history to remind ourselves of the lessons of the past. Such an exercise will encourage us to realize that the God of impossible things and insignificant people did not stop his activity with the close of the canon.

How did the modern missionary movement begin? It really started with William Carey (1761–1834), the Baptist missionary. He left his native Northamptonshire and sailed to India in 1793. His strategy of Bible translation, evangelism and church-planting, hand in hand with education and relief work, has been the basic pattern employed in world mission ever since. One biographical essay about Carey describes how he cut his teeth as a preacher by preaching in 'the pulpit of a tiny non-conformist church, a two-hour walk from his home'. God used that small church to nurture a great champion for Christ.

In fact, as we review church history, do we not see that God always starts his works small? After all, he created the world out of nothing! The Lord Jesus Christ chose just twelve disciples and from there began the church which turned the ancient world upside down. The great Reformation of the sixteenth and seventeenth centuries, which recaptured the truth of the gospel of grace for a lost world, began with one man, Martin Luther, at last coming to see from the epistle to the Romans that God freely justifies the ungodly through faith in Christ. The evangelical revival which swept across Britain and America, and changed the face of those countries during the eighteenth century, was born out of a small gathering of men like George Whitefield and John Wesley, who met as the despised 'Holy Club' at Oxford University. God likes to use the few and the nobodies.

God's use of small groups is not confined to the past. Looking back over the last twenty or thirty years I can think of places in many parts of the country where God has used small groups of people to plant works which have now become strong churches, centres of faith and life.

We need to realize that there is nothing wrong per se with being a small church. What is our attitude? Will you see your low numbers as an obstacle or as a springboard to faith that God can glorify himself through you? That is the choice to be faced.

2.
Satan's tactics against local churches

Many Christians from congregations where there are few people in attendance see their problem as being their smallness. 'If only we were bigger,' they say. 'If only we had more workers, more finance.' But actually, smallness is not a problem in itself. Reading the New Testament you will find that the number of people in a church is barely a relevant factor as to the church's usefulness to Christ, and certainly is totally irrelevant as regards its acceptability to Christ.

There is nothing wrong with being small. Every church starts small. When Paul took the gospel to Philippi, the first meetings of the church probably consisted of not many more than just Lydia the business woman, the jailer and his family, along with the slave girl from whom Paul had cast out a demon (Acts 16). From there the church grew. A baby is not said to have problems because it is not immediately as large as its mother or father.

Furthermore, sometimes God's strategy is to keep churches small. Over the last half-century, unheralded by the secular media, the world has seen perhaps the greatest revival it has known so far. In Communist China, millions upon millions of people have become Christians. Yet many of those Christians meet in small fellowships of God's people. There is a fascinating book entitled *Operation China*,[1] which details the present state of the Chinese church and provides much data about the progress of the gospel among the various people groups within that vast land. In 1994 believers from Jinghong and Mengla of Yunnan province reached out to the Jino people who live in the jungles and mountains of the area. As a result 300 people within the Jino have become Christians, and the book explains that this has resulted in thirty-one churches. Do the arithmetic for yourself to calculate the average size of those churches! They are very small. But God has raised them up and it seems such small groups are best suited to serve the people and God's purposes in that geographical location, at least at the present time.

Recently, I came across a report from *France Mission* which similarly argued that smaller churches, never exceeding forty to sixty people, are right for their situation. The report explained that there are two cultural reasons behind this. Firstly, because of bad preconceptions of Christianity based on the behaviour of the Roman Catholic Church in the past, French people are suspicious of churches that appear to be power-wielding institutions. They are more attracted to a church that is like a family, with close personal relationships. This only works where churches are comparatively small.

Secondly, the virtues of liberty, equality and fraternity of the Revolution of 1789 still mean a great deal to the French people. They like to have their say in decision-making. Having a smaller church enables people to do this, and so fits the French situation. Smaller churches can sometimes be precisely the design of God.

Diagnosing the problems

The real problems in churches are to do with a lack of life and of fruitfulness, not the fact that it is a little flock. A church may have dwindled in size because such spiritual life is missing. Smallness may be a symptom of other difficulties, but that is not the root of its problems. It is possible to see faith, love and hope overflowing in small fellowships just as much as in those that are large. The evidence of the grace of God does not depend on numbers.

Rather, the real problems in churches are always spiritual. The local church is a crucial part of God's kingdom. It is the body of Christ (1 Corinthians 12:27), through which, by his Spirit, the Lord Jesus continues to manifest his presence in the world. The local church is God's base for gospel outreach to a whole district. As such, it is a prime target for Satan's attacks. The devil wants to cause spiritual problems which will sap the church of its life and make it unfruitful.

We have said in the first chapter that small churches are uniquely equipped to bring glory to God. It is through our weakness that God's power and strength can be perfectly shown (2 Corinthians 12:9). But if a small church is going to be in a position where God can use it to reveal his glory, then it must take steps to avoid the pitfalls that Satan uses to trap churches. A church may already be ensnared by one or more of Satan's 'anti-church devices', in which case, with God's help, steps must be taken for the church to be released. These spiritual problems will make a church unfruitful or may even cause its existence to cease.

Of course, the devil attacks us as individuals. There are always temptations and discouragements to overcome personally. At that level, as Christians we are engaged daily in a spiritual battle. But the gloomy or cynical Christian can influence others within a fellowship. The writer to the Hebrews warns us to 'see to it that no one misses the grace of God and that no bitter root grows up to cause trouble and defile many' (Hebrews 12:15). The text recognizes the possibility of sin and unhelpful attitudes being contagious within a church. Additionally, in the opening chapters of Revelation the Lord Jesus addresses seven churches, and often exposes the sins each has fallen into together, as a church. He calls such churches to repent and put things right.

So, before we go any further in pursuing our encouragement for small churches, we need to clear the ground. We are going to stop and consider a check-list of some of Satan's tactics against local churches. There are many, but I am going to suggest five of which we need to take particular notice. The fact that they can all be specified by a word beginning with the letter 'd' not only alliterates with the word 'devil' but may help us to remember them and be on the look-out for them in our own fellowships. Satan's five major tactics against local churches are *deviation, division, decadence, discouragement* and *distraction*. If we find them in our church, we had better be prepared to do something about them. The living Christ, who walked among the lampstands (representing the churches) in the opening of the book of Revelation (1:20), still calls the churches to repentance.

Deviation from the truth

Heresy has always been one of Satan's primary weapons. Truth is so precious for two reasons. Firstly, it is through hearing the truth of the gospel concerning Jesus, his death and resurrection that sinners come to faith and find forgiveness and eternal life. The apostle Paul equates being saved with coming to a knowledge of the truth (1 Timothy 2:4). So does the Lord Jesus (John 8:31–32).

Secondly, having come to salvation, it is through the renewing of our thinking by God's truth that the lives of Christians cease to be conformed to the pattern of this world and are transformed to be more like that of Christ (Romans 12:1–2). Without the truth of God as we find it in Scripture, we can neither fulfil our evangelistic obligations nor live in a way that pleases God. No wonder our enemy the devil is keen to attack the truth.

There are two main ways in which we can fall into doctrinal deviation.

• *False teachings*. Classically, heresy has involved deviating from what the Bible teaches concerning the major doctrines of the Christian faith. Secularists refuse to accept that God is our Maker, Provider and Judge. Theological liberals deny the trustworthiness of Scripture and the fact of Christ's bodily resurrection. Jehovah's Witnesses deny the truth of the Trinity and in particular that the Lord Jesus Christ is co-equal with God the Father. The Roman Catholic Church, like the Judaizers of Paul's day, deny that salvation is by faith alone in Christ alone and requires no merit in ourselves. The Lord Jesus calls churches to repent of false teaching (Revelation 2:15–16).

- *Doctrine does not matter.* But the devil's tactics these days are often subtly different from those he used in previous generations. It is not so much that he introduces specific false doctrine into the churches (though he still does that), rather it is more that he insinuates the relative unimportance of truth altogether. We live in the so-called post-modern age.

Post-modernism has its counterpart in the church. Sadly, many churches now sit very loose to their confessions of faith or the doctrinal standards of their denomination. Their church members have little or no acquaintance with such documents that seek to summarize biblical truth. In small churches there is the added pressure to lower our standards of truth just because we do not want to put too many 'obstacles' in the way of people joining the church.

Frequently the justification for this state of affairs is the idea that it is not truth but experience that counts. This sentiment is often expressed by saying that it is not theology or doctrine that is important, but whether or not someone loves Jesus and has the Spirit in their heart. That sounds very spiritual on the surface, until we investigate a little deeper. When we do, we find that there is a sense in which, for example, Muslims will reverence 'Jesus'. So will Hindus. But it is not the Jesus of the Scriptures. It is not the Jesus who was God become man, who died for our sins and is now shown by his resurrection to be Lord of all. Or think of the Holy Spirit. I remember when the Toronto blessing was at its height that the *Daily Telegraph* reporter Mick Brown went to the 'Catch the Fire' conference in Toronto and found himself caught up in what had been hailed as a great move of the Holy Spirit. 'I hit the floor—I swear this is the truth— laughing like a drain,' he wrote.[2] But when he was questioned about this later, he had not become a Christian, and said that he had experienced similar things through contact with a Hindu *avatar*.[3]

The true Jesus and the true Holy Spirit are recognized through the tests of truth laid down in the Scriptures (2 Corinthians 11:3–4). Taken to its logical conclusion, to say that doctrine does not matter will mean the disappearance of the Christian faith. Instead of being duped by the line that doctrine is relatively unimportant, the New Testament calls all churches to 'contend for the faith that was once for all entrusted to the saints' (Jude 3). We must do that by distinguishing between truth which is essential to the gospel and emphases of secondary importance. We must do that with respect and love for others who differ from us, but nevertheless we must do it. In a pluralistic, multi-faith society we may not be popular. That may be one of the reasons your church might be small and despised. But it is better to be small and despised by the world than to dishonour Christ by deviating from the truth.

Division in the body

The unity of a church is meant to be a great sign of the fact that Jesus is the Christ, the Son of God. In the upper room he prayed with his disciples and asked that the true church might be one, that the world might believe that the Father had sent him (John 17:20–21). Unity is important. In past years I have sometimes stood on a doorstep trying to share the gospel with someone, and their response has been, 'Why should I take any notice of you Christians? You can't even agree among yourselves!' The subject of general church unity is a very complicated one, and is beyond our remit to deal with here. But obviously, splits and divisions in local congregations can only undermine the credibility of the gospel in a locality even more.

Our oneness in Christ is also a valuable source of strength and encouragement within a church. At a practical level we can enjoy the support of one another. When people go through sickness or redundancy the church can rally round individuals and help. At a spiritual level as well, there is much to be gained when a church is at one with each other. Some churches have a daily prayer calendar listing the church members, and it is very encouraging both to pray for others and to know that other people are praying for you. Again, it is very helpful both to preachers and to others in leadership when they know that the church members are together and behind them one hundred per cent. It is not going too far to say that where true Christian love is present, there God himself is present, for God is love (1 John 4:8, 16).

So having seen all this, two things should not surprise us. The first of these is that there are many calls in the New Testament to unity within the body of Christ, e.g. Philippians 2:1–4; Ephesians 4:3–4; Colossians 3:12–14. Secondly, it is not surprising that Satan desires to cause division in churches.

There are well-worn tactics which the enemy of God tries to use in every church. He tries to stir up conflicts between people of different personalities. He tries to cause trouble between young and old, rich and poor, married people and singles, or between the races or the sexes or different families in a church. Just as in Corinth, Satan also invests effort in getting people to champion different preachers and 'celebrities', or different understandings of charismatic gifts, and so cause tensions. Then there are matters such as Bible versions and styles of music in worship. It is amazing how many issues the devil can massage to cause friction and division in a church so that love is absent. Such problems must be faced with humility and prayer. Certainly there are issues over which we might have to separate. We cannot maintain the unity of the church at the expense of denying some fundamental article of faith or tolerating some gross sin. But in all lesser areas we are called to make every effort to maintain the unity of the Spirit in Christ's church (Ephesians 4:3).

It is worth considering the fact that there can be extra factors which might cause tension in a small church. Some little churches are struggling to even survive. In such situations there are often extra dynamics at work. If not handled carefully these can open up rifts in the fellowship.

There can be the problem of nostalgia. There may be some members who can still remember the glory days of the church of yester-year. Their outlook will not be about hope for the future but rather about trying to recapture or hold on to the past. I can vividly remember being confronted by an older lady soon after I arrived in the ministry. One Sunday she came into the vestry, with her walking stick held tightly in her hand, and closed the door behind her. She had got me alone. She looked at me with steely eyes and said, 'You won't change anything, will you?' When I was unable to give her that assurance I was rather worried what she might do with the walking stick! However, I think someone must have come in and disturbed this conference, and I escaped. The agenda of such folk is to get back to doing things the way they used to be done, and often, though not always, those old ways are no longer appropriate. Such nostalgia needs to be understood. Often these people long for the apparent security found in the past. But it needs to be confronted by asking the question, 'If the old days were so great why is the church in the low condition it is today?'

Similarly there can be the slightly different problem of those from distinct church backgrounds. Apart from the 'glory-days' members, there may well be those who have joined the church over the years from other Christian denominations or traditions (new as well as old). Their answer to the problems facing a struggling church is likely to be that the church needs to conform to the tradition in which they were brought up. Within one little church there may be four or five different traditions vying for influence as to the recipe for success. But of course, mere tradition never brings life.

Such dynamics can be used by the devil to divide, and even destroy, churches. These attacks can only be beaten through patience, prayer, wisdom, much love and repentance. The risen Lord Jesus charges the church in Ephesus, 'I hold this against you: You have forsaken your first love' (Revelation 2:4). The Bible commentator Robert Mounce comments on this forsaking of love: 'The expression includes both love to God and love to mankind at large, but seems to refer mainly to their love for one another.'[4]

Decadence among the saints

We had just begun the work of planting a church. It was actually a work of restarting a church, which through immorality involving the leadership had totally collapsed. It had caused a scandal in the local area. The building had been offered to us to start a second congregation at a time when God had blessed and we were overflowing our premises. We went ahead. When we took it over, to begin with we closed this church for six months, to make it clear to the neighbourhood that when it reopened it was a completely fresh start. The Lord blessed the endeavours and things were going very well. But a little while into the project the restarted church was approached by a cable TV company. There was a little piece of land attached to the church that would be just perfectly positioned for one of their transmission units. They were offering quite a substantial sum of money for the use of this tiny site. It would take up hardly any room, and the money would be very helpful in establishing the new church. To begin with the church replant group would be quite small and perhaps this would help by providing finance towards funding a full-time pastor. What should we do?

The opportunity seemed excellent. But having considered it, we turned it down. Why? Because we thought about the kind of TV channels which often broadcast through cable. Some of those channels broadcast very ungodly films and pornography. However much money was being offered, it was not right before God for Christ's church to be assisting (even obliquely) in the dissemination of such material. The church is called to be the holy bride of Christ. We refused the offer and the Lord has gone on to establish that congregation, and it now stands on its own feet, a fine witness to the Lord. We must do our utmost to keep Christ's church holy and separate from sin.

We may have beloved church members who fall into open sin and refuse to repent. We cannot afford to let such a situation continue. Sometimes it is done in the name of love, but the toleration of sin among the people of God is always the devil's work. It is a sure way to cause God to withdraw his blessing from a church. Often he does not do this immediately. He gives the church time to sort things out.

But allowing sin to go unchecked always damages and can destroy churches. There are two aspects to notice here.

God's judgement

Firstly, in Christ's warnings to the churches at the beginning of Revelation the toleration of sin and worldliness features very prominently and brings the Lord's condemnation. If the church at Pergamum did not take steps to repent and drive out sin from among them, they will know judgement, warns the Lord Jesus. He goes on to warn the church at Thyatira similarly (Revelation 2:20–23).

Church discipline is always a most painful and difficult process. It must always be carried out with the intention and in the hope that the offending Christian will repent and be received back with joy into the fellowship. But church leaders, even of small churches, must never flinch from seeking to keep Christ's body, the church, clean. This might seem especially problematic when people involved in financial irregularities, gossip, sexual scandal, or whatever it is, have great influence within the little congregation. Sadly, if the offender is related to them, other family members within the membership might even try to take his or her side in the church meeting, or threaten to leave the church themselves. But such threats must be faced lovingly. The church must not allow itself to be blackmailed or 'held to ransom' by the threat of withdrawals. We cannot simply turn a blind eye in order to 'keep the peace.' The church does not belong to us, but to Christ.

Spiritual blindness

The second aspect of Christ's words to the churches in Revelation which is relevant here is that he points out how the toleration of sin and worldly ways brings spiritual blindness and apathy. The wealthy church at Laodicea do not even realize that they are 'wretched, pitiful, poor, blind and naked' (Revelation 3:17). The church at Sardis, happy to live on its past reputation for spiritual life, are warned that they must, 'Wake up!' and 'Strengthen what remains and is about to die' (Revelation 3:2).

The devil knows that a decadent church will at best be a blind church and if there is no repentance, it will eventually be a dead church.

Discouragement under the circumstances

Satan is a master of depressing propaganda. He loves to discourage churches. In some small churches a defeatist attitude prevails.

Often a church's negative reputation in the surrounding community contributes to this defeatist attitude. If neighbouring churches have assigned you a bad label it can be hard to shake it off. Some helpful soul may even be declaring to other Christians something like, 'That church has the mark of Satan on it. It can never prosper.' Additionally, some folk who have left the church over the years may be helping the devil in his work. Perhaps they have gone to nearby congregations and spread horror stories about what that church 'is really like'. I have to say that if there are grounds for such stories then something needs to be done. Your church needs to repent. An apology ought to be given to those you have mistreated or wrongfully offended. But often, the stories of what your church 'is really like' are at some distance from the truth. All you can do is bring that to the Lord, and leave it in his hands.

We are going to pick up more thoroughly on the topic of dealing with discouragement in a later chapter, so we will not spend much time on this satanic strategy here.

Nevertheless it is worth noting that in his dealings with the churches at the beginning of Revelation the Lord Jesus goes out of his way to encourage his people. Even to those he accuses of sin he makes precious promises, if only they will repent and do what is right (Revelation 2:7; 2:10–11; 2:17; 2:26–29; 3:4–6; 3:11–13; 3:18–22). If the Lord Jesus is keen to encourage us, then it is good for every member of a church to learn to encourage one another.

This brings us to the last of these common tactics of Satan against local churches.

Distraction from our purpose

The 1940 Nazi invasion of Belgium during World War II carries a salutary lesson. The ground attack was to be carried out by Hitler's powerful 6th Army. However, it had to overcome a formidable barrier provided by the Albert Canal before it could be deployed effectively. The bridges across the canal and the new fort of Eben Emael had to be captured and only 500 airborne troops were available for this assault.

To compensate for the scantiness of resources, and to create as much confusion as possible, at Hitler's own instigation the Nazis dropped dummy parachutists widely over the country. The ruse worked. Distracted by reports of men dropping from the skies in many different places the Belgium army took its eye off the critical area and the two key bridges were captured intact. The 6th Army was then able to cross the canal and the Nazi victory soon followed.

Distraction is a powerful weapon of Satan against local churches. We need to be clear what we are about. All local churches have responsibilities in three directions. These are inward, upward and outward. The local church is the assembly of God's people saved and called together out of the world to serve him. *Inwardly* we are called to love and build up one another in Christ as the family of God. *Upwardly,* we are to enjoy glorifying God through the praise of our lips and the obedience of our lives. And *outwardly* we have the responsibility to declare the gospel to a lost world. All three of these must be pursued and kept in balance.

Will God accept our worship if the members of the church hate one another? What point is there in going about evangelism if any new convert would only enter a church where there is bitterness between the members and dead formalism in the services?

On the other hand, one of Satan's most subtle ploys, especially with small churches, is to distract us into concentrating all our attention on the inward and the upward, while neglecting the outward work of evangelism.

Churches which are distracted from evangelism and give all their concentration to worship or to fellowship are failing and falling churches. They are churches that have been deceived. In fact their neglect of evangelism may even invalidate their worship before God. This is especially true if the real reason behind the lack of evangelism comes down to being ashamed of the gospel (Mark 8:38).

With this conviction in my mind, it was not long after starting as their minister that I was in trouble with some members of my new congregation. The forceful older lady with whom I had crossed swords over not changing anything was one of those who was most upset. There was one Sunday when she confronted me after a service fuming with anger. 'You have turned our Old Baptist chapel', she protested with great vehemence, 'into a mission hall!' There seemed particular vehemence and disdain in the way she pronounced the word 'mission'. I said little in reply, but secretly felt 'I must be on the right lines then.'

That the local church should have a missionary, evangelistic character can be seen in many ways. The New Testament identifies the original apostles as the foundation of the church. But we know that those apostles were missionary in outlook and received the great evangelistic commission from Christ, to go into all the world and preach the gospel (Matthew 28:18–20; Mark 16:15; Acts 1:8). Any properly constructed building will have the same shape as its foundations. If the foundations of the church have a missionary shape, then so must every expression of the church. The great work of the church in Philippi is described as to 'hold out the word of life' (Philippians 2:16). One of the reasons the church in Thessalonica was seen as an exemplary church was because Paul was able to say of them, 'The Lord's message rang out from you not only in Macedonia and Achaia—your faith in God has become known everywhere' (1 Thessalonians 1:8).

We must not be diverted from the priority of making the gospel known. The old logic of a message I heard long ago still has much to commend it. 'Why has God left the church on earth?' asked the speaker. 'Nearly everything we do and strive for on earth could be done better in heaven,' he went on. 'In heaven we will worship God perfectly. In heaven we will have complete fellowship. In heaven we will be entirely holy. So why does he leave us here?' Of course, the speaker's answer was this: 'There is only one thing we can do on earth which we cannot do better in heaven and that is to preach the gospel to the lost. The Lord has left us here to be his witnesses!' Every church must give priority to making Christ known in its local area. Have you been distracted?

No use pretending

Here we have seen, not all, but some of the main ways in which the devil tries to ensnare churches and make them unfit and unfruitful for God. If we are seeking to make progress for God but are ignoring the spiritual problems then we will never get anywhere. It is no good pretending. The church leaders especially have a responsibility to prayerfully consider the state of their church.

Have you watered down the truth of God to make it more pleasing to unsaved people? Have you drifted from confessional Christian faith? Are their rifts between members of the church which you have failed to address, so that a bitter atmosphere sours your congregation before God? Have you given in to those with financial or family power within the congregation and are allowing some flagrant sin to go unchecked? Have you allowed worldliness and the spirit of materialism to infiltrate your heart, so that you are a 'lukewarm' Christian? If you as a church leader are lukewarm, how can you be surprised when your congregation is marked by lack of commitment? Preachers need to ask themselves whether they too frequently berate a congregation rather than encourage them in Christ. Have we ourselves fostered a spirit of discouragement and pessimism among God's people, rather than calling them to have faith and to 'Rejoice in the Lord always'? Are you guilty of being too afraid or too busy to take the gospel to the local homes of your area and so are no longer an effective witness for Christ?

The devil's devices can be overcome. In the place of self-humbling and surrender to Christ, we engage anew with the power of God, which is far greater than the power of the devil. When we submit our lives without reservation to God, then the power of the Lord is with us, against which Satan cannot stand.

The Gideon factor

Do not be cynical. Small churches are just the churches God can use. Remember the situation which confronted

Gideon. Israel was oppressed by the vast hordes of Midian, the number of whose camels 'could no more be counted than the sand on the seashore' (Judges 7:12). It was an impossible situation. Yet, God told Gideon that his army of 32,000 men was not too small, it was too large! 'You have too many men for me to deliver Midian into their hands' (7:2). When Gideon said that anyone who was afraid of the coming battle could return home, 22,000 men left the field. That left around 10,000 to follow Gideon. But God said to Gideon, 'There are still too many men' (7:4).

Why did God say this? It was because he did not want the victory to be attributed to anything other than his own intervention. An army numbered in thousands had too much natural strength for divine power to be displayed. The Israelites had an inherent tendency to run after other gods. That is why the Lord had allowed Midian to oppress them. He wanted to set up the situation so that everyone would see that he alone is the living God. It would be the Lord and no other who delivered the people.

Also, sinful people are so quick to take the glory to themselves. After the event, God knew there would be a great temptation for Israel to boast and ascribe the victory to their own military skill or courage or some other factor they thought they possessed. But the Lord was having none of it. He took such pains to reduce Gideon's army in order that the glory should go to him and to him alone. So even 10,000 of Israel against the vast army of Midian was too many. God whittled Gideon's army down to just 300 soldiers armed with nothing more than trumpets, clay pots and flaming torches.

It was the paucity of this force and the non-military nature of their equipment that made it the perfect vehicle for God to use in overthrowing the mighty oppressor, and for the Lord's name to be exalted.

Be on your guard concerning the devil's attacks on a local church. And do not be deceived by Satan's propaganda campaign against little fellowships. Be encouraged. Small churches have the capacity to be God's Gideon force in our days. It is through weakness that God's power can be fully shown.

Notes

1. *Operation China,* Paul Hathaway, Piquant, 2000, p.234.
2. *Saturday Telegraph Magazine,* December 3rd, 1994.
3. *Evangelicals Now,* February 1995, p.8.
4. *The Book of Revelation,* Robert Mounce, International Commentary series, Eerdmans, p.88.

3.
Love's vision

Having tried to clear the ground by addressing the need to confront underlying spiritual problems, we are now in a position to proceed with our task of writing a manifesto for a small local church in our day.

Let me say immediately that I believe there may be many legitimate ways of being a church in these days. Wherever, and however, God's people meet in regular and orderly fellowship around an open Bible with a sincere desire to hear from Christ, and obey him, we have a church. Throughout the world God's people gather in various ways. There are dear Kenyan brothers and sisters who meet for worship under a particular tree on the shores of Lake Victoria. At the time of writing another friend, a convert from Islam, is presently meeting with a group in a refugee camp in Norway. Others, in lands where persecution prevails, may meet in secret locations which have to change constantly. The early church met in the houses of various church members (Romans 16:3–5; Philemon 2), and some Christians in our own day have seen advantage in this. Today, many churches hire school or other buildings, to meet in Sunday by Sunday. The place where people meet is not a primary consideration. The church is the people of God, not the building where they meet.

The common church

However, having made that clear, I have to confess that in what follows I have one particular kind of church in mind. That is a church which meets in a permanent building in a fixed locality. The reason for focusing on this kind of church situation is not because I think such churches are somehow 'more of a proper church' than others who operate within a different framework. That is certainly not the case. I focus on the classic 'local church with a building' scenario, simply because it is still very common. This is the kind of church situation in which so many people find themselves. No doubt, there are some spiritual pundits who tell us that the day of a 'building-centred' church is over. That is not very encouraging, is it! But is it really true that the time of the building-based church is finished? Are we saying that somehow the very act of meeting in a building owned by the church precludes God from working? I think that surely would be going too far.

Often the idea that we need to change our style of church comes from people who mean well but have, it seems to me, too superficial a view of why the church in Britain is in decline. The truth about the dwindling church is not simply sociological. It is not fundamentally that we are running churches in the wrong way. The fundamental reason why the church is in decline is because at present our country (and to a certain extent the church too) is experiencing the judgement of God because of its sin (see Romans 1). The problem cannot be resolved simply by adopting a new format or style. Yes, the church must be prepared to be flexible. We must seek to be genuine, welcoming and approachable. But it is not as if people are thirsting for God and it is just the style of church that puts them off. There can be no ultimate change until God moves by the power of his Spirit. And he is able to move through churches with buildings just as much as through churches who adopt other modes of expressing their life together. What needs to be sorted out is spiritual rather than organizational.

While Hindus have their temples and Muslims their mosques, are we saying that Christian chapels and meeting places must disappear from the landscape? How is that going to help the profile of Christianity in our country? It is perfectly legitimate for some Christians to pursue different and more radical ways of being a church; it is also perfectly legitimate for those who still meet in their own building to pursue God's blessing on their own situation. So, since the church with its own building is still so customary it is to that situation that we give our attention.

What kind of vision can we build for this ordinary kind of small church?

Seeds and possibilities

There are many small groups of God's people up and down the land who at present are the remnants of churches that have dwindled. They have their own building and they are concerned for the future. They are asking, 'What can we do?' They may well feel discouraged and perplexed. Perhaps they feel that if God does not act soon, their church will close before too long. That may indeed be the case. But they must not panic. They need to stop and take stock.

Under God, these small fellowships actually have enormous potential. They can be seen as a remnant from which the Lord could yet begin a marvellous work. We long for the reclaiming of our land for Christ. These little churches might just be the seeds, scattered across our land, from which God may yet give a mighty harvest for his glory. The possibility is there.

Yet, of course, there are many churches in just this kind of condition and whose problems will not be solved easily. Many think that simply by calling some brave young preacher (and his family) to be the pastor, the church can be turned around. We thank God for young zealots who are prepared to plunge headlong into such works. Often, in his grace, the Lord does bring new life to a decaying church through such men. But, sadly, just as many good young ministers are broken by such churches. After the initial enthusiasm, they feel unable to cope, and for the sake of their sanity and the good of their family they have to pull out. Perhaps their experience puts them off from ever contemplating taking up the ministry again.

The problems that bring about the failure in these small churches that call a pastor are various. Many of them may be those we have tried to address in the previous chapter concerning the devil's tactics against local churches. However, the root of the failure often lies in the fact that church members expect the young minister to do the job more or less single-handed. They expect him and his wife to turn the church around without they themselves having to break sweat. Apart from wanting to see the pews filled, they have no shared vision for the church.

What is required is a vision of the local church that is shared and owned by the congregation and to which they all are committed. They need a shared vision that will stir the members of the church to seek God urgently, take risks and exert themselves for his glory. Then, when a brave young minister comes to help lead the flock, the church does not leave the job to him. It is seen as a work in which they are all involved, and for which they will all pull together. When people have a vision they are stirred and energized. This will then unify them and bring them together to seek God's glory in their community. The apostle Paul challenged the Philippian church to 'stand firm in one spirit, contending as one man for the faith of the gospel' (Philippians 1:27).

Changing times

William Tyndale's great vision was that the people of England should have the Bible in their own language. On one occasion he is reported as telling an antagonistic clergyman, 'If God spares my life, ere many years pass, I will cause a boy that drives the plough to know more of the Scriptures than you do.' Driven by this idea, Tyndale went to Germany for help and, though being hunted by persecutors, pursued the dream of translating and printing an English New Testament. Three years after Tyndale's betrayal and murder, in 1536, Henry VIII ordered that every church in his realm should have a Bible in English. Tyndale's England was ignorant of spiritual truth. His dream was that the Bible should be accessible and understandable to all.

People still need the truth. The good news of the Lord Jesus Christ brings eternal life and salvation. But the situation is different now. Once again the truth is not being heard by the majority of people in our nation. But this time the cause is not that the Bible is not available. It is not that the Bible is in a foreign language. You can buy an English translation in almost any bookshop. The trouble is that people are not interested. They have no awareness of their need. The great gods of this world, hedonism, consumerism and relativism, have blinded the eyes and stopped the ears of the mass of the population. These other 'gospels' hold sway across the vast majority of the population. The American novelist John Steinbeck once said, 'If you want to destroy a nation, give it too much—make it greedy, miserable and sick.' That is a fair description of our nation at the present time. It is in this general context that ordinary local churches find themselves, and it is in this context that we need to capture a new vision for bringing the truth of Christ to the people.

Our society is secular. It believes God is irrelevant. It lives only for this world. As I have said, the people are enthralled by hedonism, consumerism and relativism. *Hedonism* is the philosophy of living for pleasure in this life. It encourages people to have no higher goal in life than to tickle their five senses in whatever ways they think appropriate. *Consumerism*, the 'gospel' of the advertising and marketing industries, tells the ordinary man and woman in the street that happiness lies in being able to buy and use whatever they choose. Their purchases can be anything from a new house to a holiday, from a pornographic video to a pension plan. This is where joy is found, they are constantly told. *Relativism* undergirds these selfish attitudes. It champions the idea that there is no absolute truth outside ourselves, by which we need to guide our lives. Everything is just a matter of opinion. No religion or ideology is true. No cause or belief is ultimately worth anything. Death is the end. Therefore, we might as well live as we please. True freedom is to live for self (the self, which according to God's Word, is corrupt and sinful). Taken as a whole, these attitudes dominate the population and are very hard to break through.

Love for sinners

This is not the place to go into a full analysis of the spirit of our age, which has been called by some 'the century of the self'. However, though our situation is bad, we must not think there is nothing that the church, under God, can do.

Although the self-centred secular/materialistic outlook is very resistant to the gospel, it is nevertheless vulnerable to true Christian love. The vision local churches need to capture is about love—the love of God to mankind in the gospel, which shows itself practically in love to our neighbour.

I really need to explain two things. Firstly, I need to explain the kind of love to our neighbour that I am speaking about. Sometimes we are moved to evangelism and to seek to do good through a concern for the church. We are sad to see its decline and we want to see it built up again. But though this is an understandable reaction, it is never this kind of motivation that revives the fortunes of the church. The church is revived and made powerful when people within the church begin to have an overwhelming love, not first of all for the church, but for the lost. It is a love for those outside the kingdom. When we have a love for sinners like God's love for sinners, the love that drove Jesus to the cross, then things start to happen, even in the hardest situations.

Yet we need to go further. This love for sinners must be a spiritual love. It is possible to have a sentimental love for the lost. We see people confused and dissatisfied by the world. Perhaps we see the poor single-parent Mum struggling with her family. Or perhaps we see the elderly full of regrets and growing ever closer to their last day. Our heart goes out to them. We long to help them. We long to see them happier. Such concerns are noble and fine. But if those sentiments fall short of a desperate desire to see them saved, this love will not do. It is purely human love. Many soft-hearted non-Christians have the same love for such people and try to help them in a secular way. The love that is needed is a love like the love of God, which cannot be satisfied until we see people turn to Jesus and find forgiveness and life in him. Such love drives us to share with others the saving truth of the gospel.

I spoke to a pastor quite recently who pointed up the matter. He said that in his church he does not allow people who 'like' young people to work with young people. He does not allow people who like working with young mothers to work with young mothers. He said that he does this because if he allows those who like to work with the young or with mothers to work with them, then very often they are satisfied simply by enjoying their company. They stop there and do not have the desire to actually speak about Christ to them. Thus the work goes so far, but no further. This might be an overstatement of the point, but you can see the wisdom in it.

Such a spiritual love for the lost is not natural to us. It comes from God himself.

Secular vulnerabilities

The second matter to explain is where and why secularism is vulnerable to genuine Christian love. The secular hedonistic-relativistic-consumer outlook is a hard nut to crack, but it is weak at three significant points. Identifying these weaknesses can help us to formulate a biblical vision for the local church as the vehicle of the gospel to the glory of God, in our times. What are these weak points?

Spiritual destitution

God's Word tells us that human beings are two things at the same time. God has created us with a dual nature. We are body and soul. This is shown by many texts of Scripture. For example, the Lord Jesus warned us, 'Do not be afraid of those who kill the body but cannot kill the soul. Rather be afraid of the one who can destroy both soul and body in hell' (Matthew 10:28. See also Matthew 26:41; Luke 23:46; James 2:26). The point is that there is a spiritual side to human beings which secularism suppresses. But nevertheless it is there. This means that material and worldly things can never truly satisfy human beings. The world eventually leaves them disappointed, and spiritually destitute (Ecclesiastes 2:10–11). Whether they recognize it or not, only coming to know the Lord, for whom they were made, can bring fulfilment. Secular society is actually vulnerable at this point. This is why, though we are now more wealthy than ever, we are a less happy society than ever. Now, of course that does not mean that sinful secularized people are positively looking for God. But it does mean there is a spiritual emptiness in them, and that they will be disturbed, and maybe even inquisitive, when they come into contact with a church where there is a real sense of both the presence and the holiness of God. Bear that in mind as we try to put together a viable vision for the churches.

Moral disintegration

The idea of a secular society that is decent and law-abiding is an illusion. Our legislators, usually people with a humanist outlook, have often told us that we can relax laws and trust to people's 'good nature' to promote a free and fair society. But that is a lie and has been proved a lie over the last fifty years in the Western world. The permissive society has become a society which is disintegrating. Street crime, violence, family breakdown, personal stress and medical depression are reaching all-time records. In Romans 1:18–31, Paul explains what is going on. When we exchange God for idols and the truth for a lie God judges us by giving us over to the fruits of our own foolish rebellion. The result is that the social fabric begins to fall apart. Many ordinary people have begun to get very worried about the way their communities are becoming more lawless and dangerous places. They sense that something is wrong. They know that things are not meant to be like this, but that self-centred secularism does not have any solution. Again, therefore, at this point there is a weakness that we need to expose. The church has the opportunity of showing how things can be different, through faith in Jesus Christ.

Social isolation

This point follows from the previous one. The Lord Jesus, speaking of the last days, tells us that 'because of the increase of wickedness the love of most will grow cold' (Matthew 24:12). It is not easy to love others when selfishness and violence are on the increase. At the same time the self-centred attitudes promoted by hedonism, consumerism and relativism foster communities where people do not care much about others. Old people and the disabled tend to be the outcasts in a loveless society. Single-parent families struggle to make ends meet. Living for pleasure is fine for the wealthy, but those who are poor feel they have no hope in life, and are out of place. The consumer culture actually produces many lonely people. The cult of 'me first' easily becomes the reality of 'me on my own'. God made human beings for friendship and love. Yet these things are missing from many people's lives now. The nearest thing they have to a friend is their TV. Here, once again, is a place where a church with integrity and vision can build bridges into its surrounding community and make the good news of Christ known.

The truth in love

The Scriptures tell us that the key to communicating the truth to people is to speak the truth in love (Ephesians 4:15). Love is a crucial factor, and it is love which can still open the door for the ordinary people of our nation to hear the truth of the gospel. The vision for every local church must be a vision of Christian love.

Let us just remind ourselves of those vulnerable points in our society and see how love can, under God, unlock the fortress of the secular heart.

Inner emptiness

Secular people have an inner emptiness. They are spiritually destitute. They need to hear about God. They need to hear about the love of God, 'who wants all men to be saved and to come to a knowledge of the truth' (1 Timothy 2:3). But in a relativistic world that treats all claims to truth as matters of opinion they need to see that truth demonstrated practically. They need therefore not just to hear about God but to meet him, to sense his presence. This happens in and through a gospel church where there is love. The apostle John explains why in his first epistle. He writes, 'Dear friends, since God so loved us, we also ought to love one another. No one has ever seen God; but if we love one another, God lives in us and his love is made complete in us' (1 John 4:11–12). The secularist's jibe is 'Where is this God of yours? I can't see him!' But the implication of what John says is that although no one can see God with the physical eye, yet God can be 'seen' as Christians show love. It is among loving Christians that the Lord especially delights to dwell. He is always clearly present in us if we love one another. That being so, outsiders often sense the reality of God among a loving group of God's people. The answer to their tacit atheism may not be a clever philosophical argument. It is more likely to be an encounter with God himself through his loving people. Jesus himself, alive in the church, the body of Christ, was the dynamic secret of the early church (Acts 1:1).

Moral turmoil

The secular-consumer society is one which is in moral turmoil. Our prisons are overflowing. Our businesses and financial accounting lack honesty. Our young people are having to be treated for sexually transmitted diseases. Our neighbourhoods are no longer safe after dark. Against that background a church community where the standards of God's law are upheld in a loving, attractive way will stand out. Paul tells us that all God's commandments are summed up in this one rule, 'Love your neighbour as yourself' (Romans 13:9). Church youth clubs, for example, which, with kindness, maintain the biblical standards of behaviour will commend themselves to even secular parents. They know that their children will have fun and be safe there. They know they will not be offered drugs there. People can see through such a church that this is how society at large could be, even should be, and so there is an opening for them to take notice of the gospel.

Selfishness and isolation

The current materialistic outlook breeds selfishness in society and leaves many people feeling isolated and lonely. Here, once again, Christian love can open doors for the gospel. I was speaking at a meeting not long ago, and before I spoke I got into conversation with a dear old lady whose name is Greta. She was an Austrian Jew and she told me her story. She was in Austria as a young woman when Hitler took over in 1938. As a Jew she knew she needed to escape and she was able to get away to Britain before World War II started. Sadly, her brother did not get out and she told me that he had later died in Auschwitz. In Britain, after the war, she met and married an Englishman and they had a good life together. But when he died, Greta's life fell apart. She pondered the past and saw the terrible inhumanities of the Holocaust. She looked at a lonely and seemingly pointless future without her husband. Lonely and depressed, she contemplated suicide. On the night after her husband's funeral she got together the tablets she had in her house, lined them up on the table and was set to end her life by an overdose. She was alone in the house and it was eleven o'clock at night. It was just then that she heard a knock on her back door.

A Christian neighbour, touched by Greta's bereavement, just felt moved by the Lord to go and see her. Here was a gleam of love and care which pierced the dreadful darkness. It was through this that Greta was prevented from committing suicide and over the following weeks found peace with God. 'My neighbour led me to the Lord,' said Greta, 'and O I love the Lord now.' How many other Gretas are there in the neighbourhoods of our churches, just aching for love?

Perhaps the most well-known words of the apostle Paul are these: 'And now these three remain: faith, hope and love. But the greatest of these is love' (1 Corinthians 13:13). What makes love the greatest?

Bible commentators sometimes explain these words by telling us that though there is a sense in which there will be no faith or hope in heaven, for there all God's promises will be fulfilled, yet nevertheless heaven is a world of love. If that is so, then it is through Christian love that we can bring a touch of heaven to people who do not believe heaven exists. Perhaps they will begin to see that it does exist, and that heaven the home of love has a place for them through the grace of the God of love.

Other Bible commentators say that love is the greatest because, 'God is love' (1 John 4:8). Good though those other two virtues are, we never read that 'God is faith,' or that 'God is hope.' When Christians reach out in Christlike love to others, God is using us to display his presence and his very essence. It is through our love that people who deny God's existence can find themselves confronted with his reality. The local churches therefore need to begin by catching love's vision.

In practice

It is in the context of the vision of Christian love controlling our outlook that we can now think in practical terms of setting the direction for a small local church.

Once we grasp the vision of truth being communicated in the context of love, the whole dynamic within a church changes. Yes, perhaps the pastor and one or two others who are gifted evangelistically do carry the main responsibility for conveying the truth to people. But once we understand that the truth needs to be wrapped around in love, then it becomes clear that everyone in the church has a part to play. We can no longer see even the small church as a 'one man band'. We must forsake the philosophy of 'the gifted few'. Every church member is a vital part of the team. According to our gifts and abilities there will be something we can all do to support the work.

How can love's vision be put into practice by a little group of God's people? It is all very well to have 'airy-fairy' ideas about being a loving church, but how can they be made real? We do not have great resources, but what can we do to show the love of God and so share the gospel in our locality?

I want to suggest that any church, no matter how small, can do five things. These will form the backbone of the book and we will explore them in the following chapters. We need to focus on the church having quality presence, quality welcome, quality teaching, quality hospitality and quality prayer.

These are five practical objectives I would suggest small churches should pursue. We are going to devote a chapter to each of them, but for now here are the summary headlines for these five aims. What is the way forward? What can small churches still do? I would suggest the following:

- *Quality presence.* The love of God needs to be preached to the people in our locality in such a way that they know that the church has a genuine care and concern for the community. If all a neighbourhood sees of the church is a number of cars which drive in, park for an hour or so, and then drive away, twice on a Sunday and once mid-week, it hardly commends the love of God to them. It will hardly open doors when the church does get out with the gospel to the local homes. How can the church have a presence in the area which recommends the Lord to those in the vicinity?

- *Quality welcome.* How can we make outsiders feel welcome in a little church? It is a great mistake to try to design the meetings of the saints to appeal to the unregenerate desires of sinners. We cannot change the church to suit the world. But, surely there is some way to make those unused to church feel welcome, and not awkward, without compromising the sanctity of our meetings? As churches we tend to use a lot of words which are rarely used by non-

Christians—words like 'sanctification' or 'fellowship'. We can therefore, for example, at least do our best to make sure that we use language which is intelligible to outsiders (1 Corinthians 14:22–25).

- *Quality teaching.* God has not given us an inspired video or a holy music score. Rather he has given us a holy book— the Bible. And it is through the preaching and teaching of this living and enduring word of God that people can be born again (1 Peter 1:23). How can a small church produce quality teaching which touches the hearts of modern people?

- *Quality hospitality.* If we are too busy to spend time with people, then we are very unlike the Lord Jesus, who stopped in his tracks when he heard blind Bartimaeus calling out to him. To share the truth and show the love of God we need to be able to open our lives and our homes to people.

- *Quality prayer.* One of the most wonderful things about prayer is that it is not something that depends on numbers. Small churches can pray just as well as large churches. The power of God comes by earnest prayer. Elijah was only one man, against the 450 prophets of Baal. But it was Elijah's prayer that was answered (1 Kings 18:36–38).

Each of these objectives is prefixed by the adjective 'quality'. The quality control I have in mind is not to be impressive in a slick or worldly way. The quality we must desire is to be such that, if the Lord Jesus himself suddenly arrived at the church, he would say, 'Well done!' That is the only merit that counts.

Here then are five avenues by which love's vision can be put into practice. These paths can be followed even by a small congregation. It is to exploring each one of these avenues of love in greater depth that we now turn.

4.
Quality presence

Dr E. F. Schumacher was a brilliant economist, journalist and progressive entrepreneur who was also an adviser to the British Government. He was most famous for his best-selling book on economics, *Small is Beautiful*. Just after his death in 1977 another book, this time of his philosophical thought, was published. It was entitled *A Guide for the Perplexed*.

Written in the days of the cold war, it begins with Schumacher recalling standing in the centre of Communist Leningrad and looking at a map of the city. 'I could see several enormous churches, yet there was no trace of them on my map,' he wrote. 'When finally an interpreter came to help me, he said, "We don't show churches on our maps." Contradicting him, I pointed to one that was very clearly marked. "This is a museum," he said, "not what we call a *living church*. It is only the *living churches* we don't show."'[1] Isn't that interesting? The Communists went out of their way to hinder people from finding out about 'living churches'. It is fairly obvious that in the West today, the devil would like to do the same thing. He would like to erase gospel churches from the consciousness of ordinary people. He would want Christians, overawed by the brash and confident secularism around them, to hide away in a corner.

If in the wonderful purposes of God someone in your community did want to know about the way of salvation, would they think of coming to your church? Do people know that you are there? It may be that your group is so small that you have turned in on yourselves as a fellowship. Feeling despised by the frequently arrogant godlessness that surrounds you, comforting one another may have become your chief aim as a congregation. It is good to comfort one another, but do not let yourselves be taken off the map of your community's awareness and give the devil what he wants. Remember that what the world despises God uses.

A city on a hill

'What have we got to offer?' You may have chided yourselves with that question. I want to remind you that under God you have a lot to offer. Do not be taken in by the secular propaganda that tells you that the church is just a human institution, a club for 'religious' people, and yours is a pretty meagre one.

No, the church is a spiritual entity, in touch with divine reality. Your church's existence is owed to the character and purposes of God. Father, Son and Holy Spirit are with you.

You are the people of God (1 Peter 2:9), the temple of the Holy Spirit (1 Corinthians 3:16), who declare Jesus as Lord (1 Corinthians 12:3), and so offer the forgiveness of sins and eternal life to the world (Acts 2:38–39). In the audit of eternity there is no group which is more important in your locality.

Let that sink in a moment. What do people think are the most significant places in your community? The supermarket? The school? The pub? The doctor's surgery? In the light of eternity these places mean little or nothing. No one is going to be told the good news of Christ by the supermarket. No one is likely to find eternal life at the local hospital or the petrol station or even the mosque. It is highly unlikely these days that the headmaster or headmistress of the school will tell the children about Jesus Christ and why he came. Therefore it is right that your presence be known. Every church should seek to be Christ's 'city on a hill that cannot be hidden' (Matthew 5:14).

When we ask, 'What have we got to offer?' remember that you have the gospel. 'But there are so few of us, and our resources are so limited,' you may reply. That is probably true. But do not see yourselves and the human resources available to you in worldly terms. 'Man looks at the outward appearance, but the LORD looks at the heart' (1 Samuel 16:7). We are to be people of faith. Call to mind the story of the little boy with his five loaves and two fishes (John 6:9). There were five thousand men to be fed apart from the women and children. It seemed ridiculous. 'How far will they go among so many?' asked the disciple Andrew, Simon Peter's brother. But as what they had was put at Jesus' disposal the miracle happened. The food was multiplied. When all the crowd had eaten enough the disciples collected twelve baskets full of the pieces of loaves that were left over. Instead of a fast there was a feast. Instead of idle impotence there was a clearing up job to do. To the human eye it may look as if you have little or nothing to give. But you have the gospel and yourselves, and, in Christ's hands, who knows what might happen?

How can a little church have a quality presence for Christ in a locality? The two vital ingredients are communication and incarnation.

Communication

Writing to Timothy, who has been left in temporary charge of things there, Paul describes the local church in Ephesus as 'the pillar and foundation of the truth' (1 Timothy 3:15). The truth he is speaking about, of course, is the truth of the gospel.

So we are to imagine a large column—perhaps something like Nelson's Column in Trafalgar Square in London—with the truth placed upon the top. The truth is held up high for all to see. That is the picture that Paul has in mind for every church, large or small. Every local fellowship must make some quality attempt to hold out the good news of the Lord Jesus Christ to all in the vicinity.

Let me tell you a true story. David is a married man, in his mid-forties, with two teenaged daughters. He lives in the Midlands. He was working as a civilian for the local police control centre when he was the victim of a brutal attack by some men who emerged from a pub. He was only saved from severe injury by the intervention of passers-by. This was a traumatic experience and obviously the marks remained. Not least, David was left with the inevitable questions, 'Why did this happen?' and 'Why me?'

As he got back to normal David resumed his morning jogging. It had been part of his life as an attempt to overcome the lack of exercise which went with his desk job with the police. His daily route just after dawn took him past his local evangelical church.

As he jogged with the 'Why?' questions in the back of his mind he began to notice the posters on the front of the church building. The building had two large windows by the road, where they displayed clear, bright, gospel texts in up-to-date language. The church had a collection of these posters, so each week the text was changed. The cycle of texts would repeat about every two months or so. Someone in the church was keen to communicate the truth to those passing the building.

As David jogged by he began to take an interest. He would look out for the new posters and read them each morning. It was through this that his jogging turned into an encounter with God.

As he read the posters he began to think about what they said. His attention and interest began to grow. He read the words of Jesus, 'Come to me, all you who are weary and burdened' (Matthew 11:28). David said, 'It was as if God was telling me that I had to go into that church. "Go through those doors," God was saying.'

All unbeknown to the Christians of that evangelical church a struggle had begun in David's heart. He should go into the church and find out more. But what would that mean for his life? What would his wife and children think? Eventually, as Christmas approached, he plucked up the courage, and went with his wife to the church's carol service. 'I became a Christian that night,' said David. 'In the preacher's message, I was told to stop rebelling and come to Christ. There and then I prayed and asked the Lord to forgive me and come into my life.' Not long after, David's wife came through to faith too.

Living word

David's is a simple story but it shows us the power of the Word of God. The Bible is a living book. It is not just that we read it, very often it reads us and speaks to our deepest human needs. It is a life-giving word which is never out of date (1 Peter 1:23–25). We should have every confidence and never doubt that God is able to do great things through his word.

Therefore a church must do all it can to lift up the truth of God's Word in its vicinity. It has been said, 'The church that does not evangelize will fossilize.' Different churches will be able to do this in different ways. Here we have seen an example of the use of gospel posters. We may be able to deliver attractive brochures or gospel tracts through the doors of the local homes. We may have people who are gifted at door-to-door work. We may be able to run a course like *Christianity Explored*. Perhaps some of these things are beyond the present capabilities of the small congregation. A little church may not be able to do much, but, little church, you can do something. There are three things to bear in mind as we seek to communicate with the people of our area.

- We have talked about people knowing about the church. Clearly we will want to say something in our literature about the church itself. However, some churches say a lot about themselves and their activities and very little about the gospel. We need to get the balance right. We need to be up-front with the message of the Lord Jesus Christ. The church is just the pillar. It is the truth it holds up to the community which is the important thing.

- If we use gospel leaflets, or posters outside the church, we need to do our best to convey a fully rounded picture of what God would have us say to people. People need to know that God loves them and Christ calls them. But they need to know more. They need to know the context. They need to know that God is the Creator and that we have rebelled against him. They need to know of Christ's birth, life, death, resurrection, exaltation and return in judgement. They need to know that forgiveness and acceptance with God is through grace and not our merits. We may not be able to say all these things at once, but over time we need to try to communicate all these truths to our neighbours.

- Although we are rightly desperate to see people turn to Christ, we must not hold ourselves responsible for people's reaction to the message of the gospel. Our job is to seek to deliver the message. Repentance and faith, under God, is their responsibility, not ours. The postman has finished his job when he puts the letter through the door. He cannot be held responsible for whether or not the resident pays their bills! Yes, pray for a response. Yes, yearn for a response. But do not beat yourself if hearts are hard.

In many ways the key lies in the spirit in which we seek to communicate God's truth. We are not to be happy with a bare minimum. If we stick up a poster and leave it there for months on end until it becomes tattered and worn, what message are we conveying to those who walk by? It gives the impression that we do not really care!

The fact that in the months leading up to David's conversion the posters were changed every week, not only meant that he had more to think about, but made it obvious that the people of the church really did think that the truth is important. Even in this low-key way, everyone who took any notice as they went past the building knew that those in the church were passionate about their message and wanted to communicate it to everybody. When in that spirit even a small fellowship begins to hold up the gospel in its vicinity, it starts to become 'the pillar and ground of the truth'. Here is the beginning of a quality presence for Christ in the locality.

Incarnation

Many non-Christians accuse the message of evangelicals of being mere 'cant'. The *Concise Oxford English Dictionary* gives one meaning of 'cant' as 'insincere pious or moral talk'. Cant is to do with not practising what we preach.

The charge of mere cant could never be levelled at our Lord Jesus Christ. He did not seek to communicate the message of God from heaven by bellowing at the world through a heavenly megaphone from above. He did not send angels to write messages of God's love on the clouds while himself remaining at a comfortable distance. Rather, he came among us, and not only preached the message but also lived it out, as a man among men.

Jesus took on human flesh and blood. He became incarnate among us to perfectly represent the Father and communicate God's truth to the world. In particular, it was because the Father so *loved* the world that he sent his Son into the world (John 3:16). But the sending does not stop there. We find that having died for our sins and risen again Jesus speaks to his disciples—those first representatives of us, the church. 'As the Father has sent me, I am sending you,' Jesus says (John 20:21). As Christ not only preached the message but also came and lived out the message in the world, so we must not only preach the message but also live it out in practical ways in our communities. Only then can the message of the evangelical church be delivered from the accusation of mere 'cant'.

Social gospel?

On hearing this challenge some Christians react negatively. They fear that to engage lovingly at a practical level with the local community is the pathway to fall into theological liberalism and shrink the gospel to solely social concern. There can indeed be a danger of this, so we need to be careful.

We must not fail to preach Jesus Christ and him crucified. But the opposite extreme of saying, 'our job is to preach the gospel and not get involved in social work,' is equally wrong. To go down that track is to be very unlike Jesus. Do you remember how Peter described Jesus' earthly ministry? 'God anointed Jesus of Nazareth with the Holy Spirit and power … he went around doing good and healing all who were under the power of the devil, because God was with him' (Acts 10:38).

The separation which has come about between preaching the gospel and doing good to others is foreign to the spirit of the New Testament. I think, historically, it has come about somewhat as follows. An older evangelicalism was quite at home with adorning the gospel by good deeds. But then, in the late eighteenth and nineteenth centuries, came the rise of liberalism in the church, biblical criticism and theological scepticism. The liberals began to deny the great fundamentals of the faith like eternal judgement, heaven and hell, and Christ's resurrection from the dead. Losing the eternal perspective, their preaching truncated the Christian message. Christianity was reduced to a system of ethics concerning how to live well in this life. Thus they began to focus on such matters as social concern and justice.

In reaction to liberalism, evangelicals rightly jumped to the defence of the Bible and the gospel of forgiveness and eternal life. Such pressure came on evangelicalism during the early years of the twentieth century that we tended to retreat from society into a church ghetto whose great concern was the maintenance of the truth. But at this point we began to lose hold on the necessity of living out the gospel through good deeds in the community. Putting it bluntly, many evangelicals fell into a mindset which said, 'Social concern is what the liberals are about. We don't do that. We preach the gospel.'

But that is to be unbalanced. Biblically the gospel is of prime importance. But wherever possible we are told that we must not only preach the love of God, but back up that message by practical acts of love among our neighbours. The parable of the Good Samaritan is in our Bibles. The apostle Paul challenges us by saying, 'As we have opportunity, let us do good to *all people,* especially to those who belong to the family of believers' (Galatians 6:10).

As we look back into church history, of course, we find that many of the greatest names among evangelicals have been those who have rolled up their sleeves to help the poor and needy. For what purpose did George Whitefield, the great eighteenth-century evangelist, often take collections when he preached? It was to help finance an orphan home in Savannah. Was it not John Newton, the preacher and writer of the hymn *Amazing Grace,* who joined with William Wilberforce in the early years of the work which eventually led to the abolition of the slave trade? We think too of George Muller, the great man of prayer, who financed his orphanages in Bristol through faith in God. The list could go on.

Surely this is enough to show us that to be involved in caring for our neighbours is no betrayal of our evangelical past. Rather it is to follow in the footsteps of great men and women of God. Indeed, it is to follow in the footsteps of Christ himself. It is the way that every Christian can commend the gospel of God's love to all.

These people are good news!

It is with this agenda in mind that I find Acts 2:47 one of the most challenging verses in the New Testament. There we read of the early church in Jerusalem which was born on the day of Pentecost. We know how they devoted themselves to the apostles' teaching and to the fellowship, to the breaking of bread and to prayer. But in verse 47 we are told that not only did the Jerusalem church praise God, they also experienced 'enjoying the favour of all the people'. In other words, the ordinary people of Jerusalem were pleased to have the church among them.

Why would that be? It certainly was not because the church leaders were people-pleasers. In his Pentecost sermon Peter had been unafraid to accuse his listeners of being those who 'with the help of wicked men, put [Jesus] to death by nailing him to a cross' (Acts 2:23). There is no watering down of the facts in order to gain public support.

The fact that the apostles, under God, were enabled to perform many wonders and miracles probably had a lot to do with the church's popularity among the ordinary citizens. Relatives and friends may well have been healed. Later in Acts 3 we read of the lame man who was cured and went walking and leaping and praising God. The church was doing good among the people.

We may not be able, like the apostles, to perform miracles.

We may not be able to give sight to the blind and hearing to the deaf. But can't we do what we can to help the needy in our community in the name of the Lord Jesus Christ?

Each vicinity is different. Each locality has different people. Christians must pray and think carefully about what they can do. Is there a support group for the blind that needs somewhere to meet? Couldn't you offer them your church building once a week? Are there mothers and single parents who would really benefit from being able to come to a mothers and toddlers group? Could the church facilitate that? There needs to be a practical outworking of our faith for the good of those whom we would seek to reach with the gospel. There needs to be a kind of incarnation through us. The word of the gospel needs to be fleshed out with practical expressions of Christian love. Only then will the accusation of our message being 'pure cant' be answered.

Living in the area?

There is a lot of work attached to giving the church a quality presence in an area. Making the right kind of impact for Christ will take effort.

It will mean being available to help out with putting leaflets through doors. It means being around to help with children's clubs, or cleaning the building, or whatever. My point is that all these tasks are made a lot easier if we live within walking distance of the chapel. If every time we go to a church meeting or something needs doing with regard to the premises it requires getting the car out and travelling a distance, perhaps getting ourselves held up in traffic queues, then we are making things harder for ourselves than we need to. Further, knowing human nature, it will probably mean that many necessary things will just get left.

Living in the area of the church is in fact more crucial than many people realize. Let me give a few examples of what I mean.

Witness

One of the reasons that the churches are in decline is because many churches have become dislocated from their catchment areas. The people who worship in the building do not live in the area. If they witness to their neighbours, then to get their neighbours to church is a journey. If they witness to the people who live around the chapel, they are witnessing to people who they do not know and do not know them. In this latter case there is very little opportunity for people to be able to see a Christian's life which gives credence to the gospel. The Lord Jesus came and lived among us. He did not commute back to heaven every night.

Fellowship

If many of the church live in the local area it will mean that there will be a lot of spontaneous natural fellowship among those Christians. They will see each other at the shops. Mums will meet each other as they wait for their children in the school playground. They will find it easy to drop in and see that elderly church member who has become house-bound. Expressions of love within the church become more free and less formal. This is not only good for the church but will also have a practical effect on non-Christian neighbours and friends as they look on. Jesus said, 'By this all men will know that you are my disciples, if you love one another' (John 13:35).

Consistency

Many sociologists of religion have commented in recent years that the privatization of religious belief is a devastating problem for the church. Churchgoers live their lives in separate compartments. Work is in one compartment. Home is in another. Church life is in another. And these compartments are kept separate. What people do on Sundays may be one thing, but it does not particularly affect what goes on during the rest of the week. The practice of living in one place, working in another and going to church in another is just perfect to facilitate this privatization process. You are seeing three completely different sets of people which makes it very easy to behave differently among these different groups. When we live and go to church in the same area we take a large step towards a more integrated and consistent Christian lifestyle.

I do not believe that every church member must live within walking distance of the church. But let me be very honest; I do suspect our motives sometimes. Perhaps Christians do not want to be too closely associated with the church in the eyes of their neighbours. Perhaps Christians are more concerned to live in a nice area than they are to give every effort to supporting Christ's work through the local church. Obviously I am oversimplifying things. There are other factors to be taken into account. But why is it that so many local churches are not local?

God uses the weak

When a church, small though it be, begins seeking to hold up the truth to its community, and starts to back that up with acts of practical kindness, there is a quality presence for Christ in that place. Such churches become the kinds of congregations to which the Lord Jesus Christ would say, 'Well done!' It is his approval which we look for above all else.

How do we know when we have begun to make the right kind of impact on the local area? We know when local people begin to trust the church. When non-Christian people approach us for help at some of the most painful times in their lives we know that we are beginning to make a Christlike impact. For example, it is not an easy situation, but when a pastor is asked by a non-Christian family to take the funeral of their mother, you know that a real link has been formed. Or again, when the church youth club is asked by outsiders to take on some youngsters who are going through a particularly difficult time at home, you know that the right kind of trust is being built up.

No doubt, as we think about taking on concern to provide a quality presence for Christ in our area we feel weak. Those in small churches may be especially aware of how unimpressive and how potentially 'unprofessional' we may seem in the world's eyes. Let's do our best to do as good a job as we can. But let's remember God uses the weak and inexperienced as we put our trust in him and turn that trust into prayer and practical action.

The Lord Jesus Christ has said, 'Never will I leave you; never will I forsake you,' and he is 'the same yesterday and today and for ever' (Hebrews 13:5, 8).

Notes

1. *A Guide for the Perplexed*, E. F. Schumacher, Abacus Books, 1978.

5.
Quality welcome

The new Christian had just applied for baptism and was coming into church membership. She was sharing her testimony with the church meeting as part of the process. The preacher, rather self-centredly, was hoping that perhaps a sermon he had preached might play a key part in the story. He was feeling a little down and he thought he could do with a boost to his drooping ego. But as the tale of God's grace unfolded there was no mention of the preacher or his sermons. 'I came to the church for the first time,' she said, 'and there was such a sense of love and acceptance. I knew that God was here. It just felt so different. It was that which set me on the road to Christ.' That is how the grace of God began to work in her heart.

I have heard such testimonies on many occasions. It is very humbling for the preacher. But it is very encouraging for the church and glorifying to God! Yes, of course the message of the gospel is essential, but the welcome someone receives when they come to church is very often of enormous significance in their journey to God. As we think about a manifesto for a small church, we have to consider the way we welcome people.

'Go and tell' or 'Come and see'?

However, before we proceed any further with respect to welcoming people when they come to church I need to pause for a moment. There are a few things that need to be explained.

Firstly, of course, when I speak of people coming to church it may well be to a Sunday service, but their first point of contact with the church may be through some other event which the church has organized. It may be a harvest supper, or something else. Whatever the event is, it is the first time that people have come among the fellowship of believers.

Secondly, some Christians take exception with the focus of trying to persuade people to come to church. They feel uncomfortable with asking friends to church or church events. They feel that in some way we are not really doing what we ought to be doing by way of outreach when we take this approach. 'Did not the Lord Jesus tell us to "Go into all the world"?' they say. 'The gospel begins with "go" not with "come".' Christians who invite others to church are sometimes accused of wanting to play safe and to stay within our 'comfort zone', and they can often be made to feel rather second-class in their attempts to do what they can for Christ.

My own feeling is that this is an unnecessary argument. We find both approaches used in the New Testament. Jesus does indeed tell us to 'go and make disciples' (Matthew 28:19). But Philip invited the sceptical Nathanael to 'Come and see' (John 1:46), and the woman of Samaria told her fellow townspeople, 'Come, see a man who told me everything I ever did' (John 4:29). Some people are gifted in 'going', to make the running in getting the gospel across to their friends and neighbours where they are. That is great. But others are more diffident and do not see themselves as gifted communicators; and they feel happier to ask people to come and hear someone else who is more able in setting forth the gospel. We are not to fall out with one another over 'come' or 'go' strategies. Let us rather encourage every Christian to do what they can to make Christ known.

Thirdly, every fruitful evangelistic outreach must arrive at a 'come to church' point at some time. If we are not linking people up with lively and disciplined fellowships of God's people then we are not making true disciples. The local church is the body of Christ (1 Corinthians 12:27). The Lord gifts every new Christian in some way in order for them to play a part in the building up of the body. Our growth in grace has much to do with learning to love and work with other Christians in the church. In the local church we are to pastor one another and watch over each other's souls (Hebrews 3:12–13). Without the church we are not following the New Testament pattern of evangelism (Acts 14:21–23). So whatever our method of outreach there must come a time when people cross the threshold of the church for the first time.

Whether people come by invitation, or, as often happens, whether they wander into the church of their own accord, the church needs to give a quality welcome to people.

How the gospel affects our welcome

We often see the words on church leaflets or notice boards which tell us that 'all are welcome'. But do we mean it? Is everyone, of whatever background, welcome in our church? This is where we have to begin.

Many who have been involved with higher education will, I suspect, have had experience of the following situation. At the beginning of the university year there is usually a 'societies fair'. All the different societies and clubs within the university have a stand and try to get new students to sign up. The breadth of things a new student can join is quite amazing, from political societies, to sports clubs, to theatre groups, to choirs— the list is endless. But many a new student's experience is that having signed up during 'freshers' week for the drama group or whatever, they get little further. When they attend the first meeting of the society, it becomes quite obvious that there is an 'in-group' who know one another very well and the new boy or new girl is not really wanted. They never bother to go to the drama group again. A first-time visitor to many churches has exactly the same experience.

Furthermore, it is not just that Christians can be cliquish. There is anxiety on the part of the newcomer. It is a big matter, especially for a non-Christian, to cross the threshold of a church. How do we make Christians understand this?

I heard that an experiment like the following took place at one Christian seminar. It was a seminar which concerned outreach to the lost. The Christians came into the seminar room and there was the speaker at the front of the class. The attendees sat down at desks, and to their surprise they found not just some paper and a pen with which to make notes, but also a one-pound coin. What was that for? The speaker told them they would get to that later. The morning proceeded well with much teaching and discussion.

Then the speaker explained about the one-pound coins. 'As an experiment for you to feel the kind of emotions which might go through a non-Christian's system on entering the alien culture of church I want you to do something,' he said. 'I want you this lunch time to take that one-pound coin and go down to the local book-makers and place a bet on a horse race.'

I expect there was stunned silence. Christians don't bet. (That is right and they should not.) 'I've never been into a betting office. I would not know where to start or what to do,' thought one of the participants. 'What if I make a fool of myself? To be *seen* going in there! What might people think?' thought another. Slowly it began to sink in, that it is just like that for many non-Christians if they pluck up the courage to go to a church service for the first time. They are handed a hymn book, but they are not used to singing. They find a Bible in the pew, but do not know how to find the reading in Lamentations, or wherever. What do you do if the collection box is passed around and you have no cash with you? It really entails crossing a boundary from one culture to another.

Whether anyone went to place a bet I do not know. I could not encourage betting. But I thought the seminar speaker had hit on something that made Christians aware of the kind of culture-shock many non-Christians face in coming to church. Once we realize what a huge step it is, of course, we will want to do all we can—within the bounds of godliness—to make them feel wanted and welcome. It is the gospel itself which prepares us and enables us to be good 'welcomers'. There are two aspects here.

Treat everyone the same

First, as we read through Matthew, Mark, Luke and John it is quite clear that Jesus was an approachable person. He did not limit his friendship to the religious and the respectable. It was this fact which often made him unpopular with the Jewish leaders and Pharisees of his day (Mark 2:16; Luke 15:1–2). In fact Jesus seemed to go out of his way to befriend the outcasts and problem people of society. He took interest in Zacchaeus the despised tax-collector who collaborated with the Roman oppressors. He spoke to the Samaritan woman at the well. She was not only a woman of a race the Jews despised, but she also had quite a chequered history. The man possessed with a legion of demons, who was totally uncontrollable by his community, Jesus made a bee-line for. Little children, who were counted as of negligible importance in first-century society, were those that Jesus made time for and blessed. Without in any way compromising his holiness Christ even found kind and encouraging words for the woman taken in the act of adultery. It is true that all were welcome with Jesus. His explanation was that it is not the healthy but the sick who needed his skills as a physician of souls (Mark 2:17). If our church is to follow in the footsteps of Jesus, then we must by God's grace put aside all prejudices and class distinctions and have a place in our hearts for all.

Treat others as better than ourselves

Secondly, we will only attain this humble and welcoming attitude if we truly let the gospel do its work in our own lives. Church people are often accused of giving the impression to outsiders of being 'holier than thou'. Sometimes that is an unfair smear. But sometimes there is truth in it. Because we are saved rather than lost, we can foolishly fall into thinking that we are better than other people. But we are not. Salvation is not by merit. It is by God's grace alone and we ought never to forget that. Paul's testimony was that 'Christ Jesus came into the world to save sinners—of whom I am the worst' (1 Timothy 1:15). Unless, like Paul, we see ourselves as the worst of sinners, we will find that we carry an air of somehow being a cut above other people. This will strike a death-blow to a truly welcoming attitude.

Broadly speaking, modern Christians do not like to be reminded of their sins. But it can be good for us. Properly handled, being reminded of our sins can humble us and make us more ready to see others as better than ourselves. It can make us more able to accept other people as they are. If we truly have grasped the sinfulness of our own hearts and the wonder of the love of God, then when we see others we are tempted to look down on we will think again and remind ourselves, 'There but for the grace of God go I.' Then we will see others as fellow sinners with us. They are part of the brotherhood of man. They have the great dignity of being made in the image of God. They have the privilege of being loved by God even though they, like us, are inveterate rebels against him. They are fellow spiritual bankrupts with us. We then find ourselves welcoming people in a completely different and humble spirit.

There is a vast difference between being tolerated and being welcomed. Because they are different and do not know the Christian culture, many non-Christians can feel tolerated in church rather than warmly wanted. But when the gospel of 1 Timothy 1:15 takes hold on us, we find that we become channels for the love of God towards non-Christians. We find that we really are interested in them. We find that we do have time for them. We find ourselves welcoming them as precious people.

When the gospel is allowed to shape our attitudes like this we will find that almost automatically we will avoid the errors of which the apostle James warns us. We will not be more concerned to welcome the rich than the poor (James 2:1–4). We will not be more anxious to make the well-dressed feel at home, than we are the old tramp. We will not pay more attention to the young than the old, or the beautiful more than the ugly. Each one is precious.

Love like a fire

The members of a small church can love one another just as much as the members of a larger congregation. In fact there is an argument that the members of a smaller fellowship have the advantage over the bigger church here. In a larger church, there are often so many people coming and going that it is not possible to get to know people in any depth. Relationships remain superficial. In a smaller church there is the opportunity to know one another better and so the roots of love have more depth. A small church can love one another, and if that love is healthy it will not be inward looking, but will show itself in the welcome we give to outsiders.

That sense of love can be so attractive. The secular world can be a very cold place. There are many people who are lonely and friendless. There are many others who have friends, but realize that their friends only want them for what they can get out of them. They too are disillusioned by 'cool' society. But in a church where there is genuine Christian love, which values people for what they are as made in the image of God, there can be real warmth. The love of the church can be like a fire amid an icy landscape. Such a church draws people in to enjoy its heat.

It should not surprise us that a loving fellowship of God's people is such a potent force for Christ. We live in a culture of 'implicit atheism'. People are brought up to be sceptical. 'Show us your God,' they say. 'Let us see him.'

The New Testament has a surprising answer to that request. The apostle John says on two occasions, 'No one has ever seen God.' His first response to tacit atheism is to point people to Jesus. 'No one has ever seen God; but God the One and Only, who is at the Father's side, has made him known' (John 1:18). In some ways we would expect this answer. But John, as we have noticed before, has a second response in his first letter as he writes to Christians. 'No one has ever seen God, but if we love one another, God lives in us and his love is made complete in us' (1 John 4:12). What an extraordinary response to our society's scepticism! John is saying that though people have never seen God, if we love one another, they will meet him in us and know his love through us! It is no wonder that so many testimonies of conversion, like the one I referred to at the beginning of the chapter, include a sense of the presence of God through the loving fellowship of God's people. It is just an outworking of what John is teaching in his first letter. God is love and where his people truly love one another, God's presence is manifest.

The great encouragement here is that John does not specify that a church has to be of a certain size before this manifestation of God in his love can occur. Through loving one another the presence of God can be just as real in a small group of Christians as in a larger group.

A serious but telling illustration of the impact of just one loving Christian comes to mind. At the end of 2002 the news media carried the story of an attack on the Christian hospital at Jibla in the Yemen. Yemen is a fiercely Muslim country, but the hospital had brought great good to many local people. A man entered the compound with a gun secreted in his clothing. Once inside he opened fire and three Christian doctors, including Dr Martha Meyers, sadly were killed. What was so interesting was the story which later emerged about the gunman. He was a fanatical Muslim but, some time before, he had taken his wife to that hospital. She saw Dr Meyers who had worked at the hospital for many years. It seems that when she got home from her hospital visit the wife had markedly changed and was somehow joyful. Asked about this, she told her husband that she had never been so well treated before. She felt loved and valued for the first time as a human being. 'From that time on,' in effect the murderer told the court at his hearing, 'I knew that Dr Meyers had to die. She was too dangerous a threat to Islam.' What a statement of the potential impact of Christian love that is! The wife only met Dr Meyers once, and yet her Christian kindness had such a remarkable effect.

Being yourself

We need to love people. We need to welcome people. But there is a danger of trying to impress people. If we fall into the trap of trying to impress then we have gone astray. The impressive house is right next door to the house of falsehood, and God himself cannot enter or be glorified there.

We need to learn to welcome others while at the same time being ourselves. We need not put on any airs or graces. Trying to impress belies a feeling of insecurity in us. We want to impress because we are so aware of how small our church is and we would feel much better if our congregation were more numerous. Hence our welcome does not come from genuine Christian love but from an 'enlightened self-interest' which flows out of our own need to feel more worthwhile and secure. We need to confront this in ourselves and repent of it. Our security is in Christ. We have nothing to prove and nothing to lose if our trust is in the Lord. He is our rock and our fortress (Psalm 18:2), in whom we take refuge. There are a number of practical things to say here.

- If we try to make out that we are what we are not it will not take long for visitors to sense that we are pretending. This will be counterproductive. It may well leave them with the impression that there is more wrong with the church than just the fact that it is small. 'Why are they doing this? Is there something else that they are trying to hide?' These may well be the thoughts in a visitor's mind.

- If people come along to church and there are only a few present, there is a tendency to feel embarrassed by the lack of numbers. But that feeling of embarrassment often has its roots in wanting to be impressive. Rather, we need to welcome people with a genuine love for them. We might even say something like, 'There are not too many of us, but I hope you will feel at home here.'

- You are a small church, so do not try to operate as if you were not. The Lord knows you are small and he still values and loves you. When a church has dwindled, but still occupies the main sanctuary with the preacher addressing a few listeners from some distant pulpit there is a sense of unreality about the situation. This again is likely to make visitors feel awkward and give the appearance that the church is somehow in denial. Why not instead capitalize on the positives of being a small group? Move to a smaller room. This may well bring a more intimate and relaxed atmosphere to the church. A little congregation can have a closeness and a reverent informality which is very attractive to outsiders.

Do your best to welcome folk, but do not be too disappointed if some do not come again. People make decisions for all kinds of reasons. Some Christians will not come back to a little church because they realize that to become a member in a small church would involve a lot of hard work. They are looking for a larger church where they can simply be 'passengers'. Their unwillingness to return says more about them than it does about you.

Some non-Christians will not return. Some will be offended by the gospel. We cannot help that. We must love them and welcome them, but we cannot change the truth for them. Like the Lord Jesus with the rich young man, we will have to love them and let them go. Sometimes people are offended for the most trivial of reasons. Not long ago I had a first-time attender walk out of the church. On enquiry through a third party, I later found she had decided to leave because the preacher (me) was not wearing a gown and a dog collar. Well, if I dressed to suit her, I think I would probably lose 90% of our regular congregation. You cannot please everyone. You just have to pray and lovingly leave such folk with the Lord.

The welcome that heals

The love of a small fellowship can be so helpful. You never know who may come through your doors. One young woman I know was brought up in a fairly large church in the north of England. When she was around eleven or twelve years old a man with fresh ideas became the new minister. Sadly it ended with the church splitting. This was a great shock to her young faith. The new minister took off a large group of people and left. The girl's parents were among those who stayed behind with the despised 'old guard.' She, meanwhile, soldiered on in her faith. The church began to get back on its feet and eventually she went off to university. There she got involved in a good Bible teaching church and grew as a Christian. But on leaving university she had to depart to another part of the country to start her first job. She was away from home and finding it difficult. Then came the shattering news. Her home church had split again! This greatly disillusioned her. She became cynical. For six months she did not go to church at all. She felt like giving up on Christ altogether.

But in her desperation, she found a tiny church where there were only around twenty-five people. Here she found a real welcome. Here she found no church power struggles or politics. 'They were just a small group of loving people,' she said. And that small group of Christians were such a tonic for her spiritual life. Their humility and kindness were like a medicine her soul needed to nurse her spiritual wounds. That small church cured her of her cynicism and disappointment and brought her back to stability and joy in Christ. The love of a little church can do great miracles.

6.
Quality teaching

Preaching to a small group of people can, surprisingly, have its positive side. Edward Payson was a great American Congregationalist minister of a former era. I have read the story that one storm-swept Sunday he made his way to the place he was to preach to find there was just one person in the church. Nevertheless Payson preached his sermon as carefully and as earnestly as if the chapel had been filled with earnest listeners.

Some months later the one man who had been there went to see Payson. 'I was led to the Saviour through that service,' he told him. He explained further how it had happened: 'For whenever you talked about sin and salvation, I glanced around me to see to whom you referred, but since there was no one there but me, I had no alternative but to lay every word to my own heart and conscience!'

I suppose what I have to say in this chapter is meant largely for pastors and lay preachers who regularly bring the Lord's message to a little flock. I hope that the story of Edward Payson encourages you. In a small church the preacher has the opportunity to look the people in the eye and address each person in a much more direct way. We should never despise the opportunity to teach and preach to small groups.

The one place in the New Testament where there does seem to be a direct reference to the small size of a local church is found among the letters to the seven churches in Revelation. Here the glorified Lord Jesus Christ addresses the church at Philadelphia (we are going to look in more detail at what Jesus says to this church in the last chapter of the book). He says, 'I know your deeds. See, I have placed before you an open door that no one can shut. I know that you have little strength, yet you have kept my word and have not denied my name' (Revelation 3:8).

The commentator Robert Mounce writes concerning this verse, 'Christ recognises that although they have little power (it is probably a fairly small congregation and they had not made a major impact on the city), they have faithfully kept his word and not denied his name.' But the point is that small churches, just as much as large fellowships, can promote sound teaching and Christ is pleased with that.

A trap to avoid

Sound doctrine is good (Titus 1:9; 2 Timothy 4:3). But there is a pitfall to avoid here. Some small churches and pastors of such churches take up the idea of quality teaching but they do so in a wrong spirit. They seize upon it in a rather fractious and bitter way.

When they teach they always seem to be gunning for somebody. They appear to take delight in going out of their way to criticize the charismatics and the Arminians and modern hymns and home Bible studies and the Alpha course and Anglican evangelicals and ... on and on it goes.

If you listen carefully you can pick up the subtext of what they are really preaching. Their true concern is about justifying their own ministry and their own existence. Now sometimes, of course, there is a need to correct false ideas; but when this becomes the staple of every other sermon, do you see what is happening? Actually, subtly, we are preaching ourselves. We have become self-advertisers. We are telling people that we are the church they should attend because all others are faulty. And it is amazing how adept we can become in spotting the problems in other people and congregations.

But this is not what we are meant to be about. What does the apostle Paul say? 'We do not preach ourselves, but Jesus Christ as Lord, and ourselves as your servants for Jesus' sake' (2 Corinthians 4:5).

Quality teaching does not mean that we shirk the responsibility to defend the flock and denounce heresy when we have to. But it does mean that we concentrate on the glories of Christ and the gospel. Small church, does the thunder and lightning from the pulpit flash most often against other Christians rather than your own sins and shortcomings? If so, you have fallen into the pit of self-righteousness and judgementalism (Matthew 7:1–5). Small church, at the end of each service, are you left wondering at the fragrance of free grace, the profundity of God's love at Calvary and the assurances of God's infallible promises to the lost? Or are you rather left wondering how anybody except someone who attends your church could possibly be saved? If it is the latter, then something is dreadfully wrong.

Sound teaching is first and foremost about finding Christ in all the Scriptures (Luke 24:27), and pointing everyone to him.

Sound teaching

We are evangelicals. We are, I hope in the right sense, proud to be called evangelicals, because that word comes directly from the New Testament Greek word for 'gospel'. As evangelicals our teaching is the gospel of the Lord Jesus Christ which we find in the Bible. We need to be clear about what our message should be.

The label 'evangelical' started to be used around the time of the Reformation when first John Wycliffe in England and later Martin Luther in Germany looked at their Bibles and woke up to how far the Roman Catholic Church had drifted from the original teaching of Jesus and the apostles. Later the description 'evangelical' was attached to the great revival movements of the Holy Spirit in Britain and America in the eighteenth and nineteenth centuries. Preachers like John Wesley, George Whitefield and Jonathan Edwards were mightily used of God to see thousands of people thoroughly converted to Christ. During this time the whole spiritual and moral tone of these nations was lifted. The men and women of the Reformation and revivals were gospel people, 'evangelicals'.

The term 'evangelical' is used to label a theological position, a body of truth which evangelicals believe is of first importance to the Christian faith. There is a sense in which, of course, our message is everything which the Bible teaches. But it is helpful to have the main thrust summarized in our thinking. We need a definite idea about those things which are of first importance. We are going to use a text from Paul's first letter to the Corinthians, to set out the essentials of the gospel and therefore the main thrusts of quality teaching within a local church.

> Now, brothers, I want to remind you of the gospel I preached to you, which you received and on which you have taken your stand. By this gospel you are saved, if you hold firmly to the word I preached to you. Otherwise, you have believed in vain. For what I received I passed on to you as of first importance: that Christ died for our sins according to the Scriptures, that he was buried, that he was raised on the third day according to the Scriptures, and that he appeared to Peter, and then to the Twelve (1 Corinthians 15:1–5).

Authority

At root, when the term 'evangelical' is used, one central issue is in view: the issue of authority. How do we decide what is true about God? By what authority do we make up our minds what is right or wrong for our lives? This is the question.

The evangelical's answer is 'by the Bible'. To be an evangelical is to be a Bible man or a Bible woman. There is a repeated phrase which Paul uses as he reminds the Corinthians of the true gospel. It is the phrase, 'according to the Scriptures'. Christ died and rose again, as the Old Testament had said he would. Paul looked upon the Bible as the word of God, through which God reveals his truth, and so should we. The Bible is our authority because it is the God-breathed record of Jesus, which shows the way of salvation and contains all that is necessary to thoroughly equip us to be men and women of God (2 Timothy 3:15–17).

Of course, many people do not agree with the idea of taking the Bible as our authority. Historically, in the Western world, people have basically proposed four different answers to the question of authority. These are the Bible (the evangelical position), the church, experience and human reason.

- 'Yes,' said the Catholic Counter-Reformation, 'we need the Bible, but only the church has the authority to tell you how to interpret the Bible.' It was as if the Bible was there, but only the church could provide you with the right spectacles with which to read it. In practice this meant that real authority passed from the Word of God to the popes and prelates of the Catholic Church.

- 'No,' said the eighteenth-century philosophers of the Enlightenment, 'we do not need the Bible or the church.

Human reason on its own will give us all the answers we need.' But as time has gone on we now know that is not true. Human reason will give you different answers depending on what assumptions you make in the first place. If you assume that the good of society as a whole takes priority over the good of individual human requirements, then reason will lead you to a form of Communism. If you assume the opposite, human reason will lead you to a form of capitalism. Every one of us has our own assumptions and reasons, and the philosophy of the Enlightenment has led us into post-modernism, ending up with no authority at all.

- 'No,' said the Romantics of the nineteenth and twentieth centuries, 'real truth comes not from reason, but from personal experience. What you feel deeply, that is what is true.' But with such an outlook the best you can hope for is to find 'what is true for you'. Though it might be true for the individual, it carries no authority with anyone else. Once again this path leads us into a philosophical *cul de sac*.

- 'No,' says the evangelical, 'you are all wrong. The Bible alone is our authority, for it is the word of God and not of men' (Mark 7:8). The fact, for example, that Christ died and rose again, according to the predictive prophecies of the Old Testament Scriptures, attests the fact that the Bible really is the word of the eternal God. As we prayerfully seek God, he gives us the help of his Holy Spirit, so that we can read and understand the Bible for ourselves. God speaks through his word. This is the position of the evangelical.

Yes, we listen to the traditions of the church. We can learn from other people and from history. Yes, we use our reason. After all, it was God who made us with a mind. Yes, we are affected by our experiences. It often throws new light on a situation. But on any one issue it will be the Bible which has the final say. Like Jesus and the apostle Paul, the evangelical accepts the Bible as his authority, sufficient to guide him into truth in all essential matters of faith and conduct.

Now because that is our initial position, it means that evangelicals give prominence to certain truths, because they are central to the Bible's message. They are truths, in Paul's terms, which are of 'first importance'. Others may reject or neglect these vital doctrines, but evangelicals *hold firmly* to them, come what may.

The doctrine of Christ

Paul explains that *Christ* died for our sins. He does not at this point call him Jesus, but Christ. Along with all the historic creeds of the Christian church, evangelicals believe that though Jesus was a real human being, he was also much more than a human being. He was and is Christ.

The word Christ comes from the idea of being anointed. Just as the prophets, priests and kings of the Old Testament were chosen by God and anointed as a sign of being set apart for their particular work, so Jesus is the anointed one of God, carrying through all the plans the Father has for the salvation of the world. This makes the Lord Jesus utterly unique. He is not one among many Saviours. He is the one mediator between God and man (1 Timothy 2:5).

He is such a wonderful and mysterious person that historically it took the church the first eight centuries of its existence to fully formulate an understanding of who Jesus is. However, the essentials of theology concerning Christ can be summed up in a simple sequence of numbers. These are 2, 1 and 0. We will be on the right lines of Scripture concerning Christ if we remember he has 2 natures, in 1 person with 0 sin.

- Christ has *two natures*, he is both fully God and fully man. He is a human being but he is also God, the Son, the second person of the Trinity (John 1:1, 14).

- Christ is *one person*. His two natures do not make him schizophrenic. Even Bible passages that refer to both his natures use singular pronouns, never plural (Philippians 2:5–11).

- Our Lord Jesus Christ, though fully human, had *no sin*. He was and is a perfect human being in the sight of God (Luke 1:35; 1 Peter 2:22).

These truths are great mysteries, but because of them Jesus is thoroughly furnished to be our Saviour (2 Corinthians 5:21). The truth of the identity of Jesus is of paramount importance. He is the Christ.

The doctrine of human sin

Paul tells us that the reason Christ died was *for our sins*. It is not a nice place to begin, but the whole message of salvation in Scripture is made necessary by one thing—sin. Though human beings were made perfect originally, in the image of God, yet all mankind has fallen into sin and become rebels against God. What does the Bible tell us about sin?

- Sin is *universal.* Scripture teaches us that 'all have sinned and fall short of the glory of God' (Romans 3:23). All human beings, apart from Jesus, are sinners.

- Sin is *original.* Since the first man Adam rebelled against God sin is endemic to us. It is like a genetic disease with which we are all born (Psalm 51:5).

- Sin is *total.* The Bible does not teach that we are as wicked as we possibly could be. But it does teach that every single aspect of our humanity—body and soul—is affected by sin (Ephesians 2:3).

- Sin is *fatal.* 'The wages of sin is death' (Romans 6:23). Sin puts us very much in the wrong with our holy God. It exposes us to his eternal judgement and condemnation.

Although, as made in his image, we are precious to God, yet every one of us, in our sin, is totally unacceptable to God. We are guilty and heading for hell.

Of course, that is not popular teaching. People find it insulting. It is not the kind of message which modern pop-psychology, with its concern to affirm people, would want us to convey. 'You must encourage people,' it would say, 'not make them feel guilty and call them to repent.' It is a truth which provokes disapproval. But nevertheless it is a truth which people need to hear. For if people do not understand that they are sinners, they will not understand why they need a Saviour—the Lord Jesus Christ. So, despite its unpopularity, evangelicals have stood by the doctrine of human sin as a truth of first importance.

The doctrine of penal substitution

Paul explains to the Corinthians that *Christ died for our sins*. When Jesus died, he died in our place (as a substitute), bearing the penalty we deserve for our sins. So it is that evangelicals have spoken of Jesus' death as a 'penal substitution'.

Let me talk in individual terms for a moment. The real problem is not how my sin affects me, but how it affects God. Though God loves us, sin inevitably brings about the holy reaction of his righteous anger. So when Christ died on the cross he was not doing something first of all to change me. Rather he was satisfying God's holy justice for sin. He died in order that God might be able to see that justice is done for my offences, while at the same time being able to forgive me. In the words of Scripture, Jesus died in order that God might be 'just and the one who justifies those who have faith in Jesus' (Romans 3:26). By the death of Jesus as our penal substitute we are saved.

So it is that the cross becomes the central feature of the Christian faith. Jesus instituted the communion service at which we remember, not his life, not his resurrection, but 'the Lord's death until he comes' (1 Corinthians 11:26). The apostle

Paul shows the same priority. He will not boast in anything at all except the 'cross of our Lord Jesus Christ' (Galatians 6:14). That is why the cross has always been the primary emblem of the Christian church. The evangelical understands this and cherishes the penal substitution of Christ at Calvary, above all else.

Sadly, this great doctrine is under attack today from many directions. Some people call the cross immoral. 'How could God think it was right to punish an innocent third party (Jesus) and so let us off for our sins?' they protest. 'How would it be right, for example,' they say, 'for a judge to punish your brother for your crimes?' With such arguments they reject penal substitution.

But what they are saying is actually a caricature which misunderstands the Bible's teaching about the cross. There is a very well-known verse in Romans which says, 'God demonstrates his own love for us in this: While we were still sinners, Christ died for us' (5:8). This verse is actually quite odd. This is seen if we remove the names God and Jesus, and replace them with the names (say) Peter and David. It would now read, 'Peter demonstrates his own love for us in this: While we were still sinners, David died for us.' That would not make sense. How could David's death demonstrate that Peter loved us? No, Romans 5:8 does not make sense unless God and Christ are essentially one and the same. (This is, of course, what the Bible teaches in the incarnation.) God was not punishing an innocent third party at the cross. Rather he was stepping into our place in the person of his Son and paying for our sin himself! This is the marvel of the good news of the gospel.

Evangelicals can face the problem of sin honestly and squarely, because we have a strong doctrine of the atonement. Sin is terrible, but the cross of Christ is marvellous! This is of first importance.

The doctrine of justification by faith alone

Paul tells his Corinthian readers that 'by this gospel you are saved, if you hold firmly to the word I preached to you. Otherwise you have believed in vain.'

The great thing is to receive the gospel with faith and to go on believing it. Faith is essential. This is the key to the personal question, 'How are *my* sins forgiven?'

For all their wide diversity all religions can be divided into two camps. In one camp are the religions which say 'Do'. But over the second camp we find the motto, 'Done'. Religions in the 'do' camp stress what they say we must do to be acceptable to God, or attain the divine.

- There are *mystical* religions. These propound various disciplines and techniques for attaining spiritual experiences of different kinds.

- There are *ritual* religions. These tell the seeker to go to priests and priestesses and to perform any number of liturgical and cleansing ceremonies which are said to gain access to God or the divine.

- There are *ethical* religions. Here a person will be instructed in all kinds of moral laws and charitable deeds which it is said will bring merit before God and so make him or her acceptable to God.

Obviously among all the religions and cults in the world there are those which are a mixture of these with various proportions of the mystical and the ritual and the ethical strands. However, whatever the different ideas and techniques, the point is that they all tell us to 'do' something.

In the other camp there is just one faith. The Christian gospel does not say, 'Do' it says, 'Done.' Christianity alone tells us that God is so holy and we have fallen so far that there is nothing we can do. But it goes on to tell us that all has been done for us by Christ. This is the point of the resurrection. The Bible says that the wages of sin is death, but because Christ had received and dealt with all the wages which our sin deserved, he rose again on the third day. Death could no longer hold him. The cross is the payment for our sins and the resurrection is the receipt. The resurrection was God's way of proclaiming that all that needed to be done to put sinners right with himself had been done by the Lord Jesus. 'Christ died for our sins according to the Scriptures … he was buried … he was raised on the third day according to the Scriptures.'

There is total salvation in Christ and it becomes ours as a free gift. We contribute nothing. It is a sheer gift we receive by faith. The old hymn is right when it tells us,

The vilest offender who truly believes
That moment from Jesus a pardon receives.

That is the marvellous truth of God's grace, and evangelicals see this as of primary importance in all that we preach and stand for as churches.

The doctrine of conversion

Becoming a Christian inevitably involves a changed life. As Paul writes to the Corinthians, he reminds them of 'the gospel I preached to you, which you received and on which you have taken your stand'. They were not what they used to be. Their lives now had a totally new foundation—the gospel.

Evangelicals have never been 'universalists'. They have always been 'conversionists'. There must be conversion to Christ. Not all will be saved; only those who turn to follow Christ will be saved. For people to remain as they are is for them to be lost in their sin. They must personally turn to Christ.

Once again, this is not a popular doctrine today. We live in days of pluralism. We are told that all paths lead to God. We live in times of a 'live and let live' philosophy. If it believes in God at all, our society assumes that more or less all those who die go to heaven. But that is not what the Lord Jesus taught. He taught that 'no one comes to the Father except through me' (John 14:6). People must turn to Christ to be saved.

• From the *human perspective* conversion to Christ involves repentance and faith (Mark 1:15). Confronted with the guilt of sin and the love of God in Christ we must call people to change. They must repent of their sin—turn from their old life and submit to serve God. They must believe the gospel—put their trust, not in their merits or abilities, but in Christ as their Lord and Saviour.

• From the *divine perspective* conversion to Christ involves new birth by the Holy Spirit (John 3:3). The life of God must come into our souls, enabling us to know God and by the Spirit's power to live for him (1 Corinthians 6:9–11).

This again is a primary truth which is non-negotiable for evangelicals. It is an essential part of quality teaching within a local church.

The doctrine of the Second Coming

Why was it so necessary that *Christ died for our sins*? The answer is because according to the Scriptures he is coming again to bring God's judgement day to the world. The risen Christ will return in glory. This will mean heaven and eternal joy for the saved. But it will mean hell and eternal punishment for the lost (Matthew 25:46).

Yet again this is a truth which is mocked and rejected and ridiculed today by many. Evangelicals have often differed over the precise details of how this will happen. There are different theories based on Scripture. There is the pre-millennial understanding, the a-millennial understanding, and the post-millennial understanding. But though we may disagree on the details we have always been unanimous about the certain fact of Christ's Second Coming (1 Thessalonians 4:16). And this is a truth which has always motivated evangelicals to mission and to evangelism. We must take the gospel of salvation to the whole world before that great day arrives.

Though Paul does not mention this specifically in the passage we have quoted, it is assumed behind what he is saying. Also, further on in chapter 15 of 1 Corinthians, he specifically mentions the end which the Lord's return will bring and some of its implications (1 Corinthians 15:24, 52). It is with this in mind that he tells the Corinthian Christians to 'stand firm' and 'let nothing move you' (1 Corinthians 15:58). So this doctrine too we may legitimately see as of primary importance.

Here then we have a thumbnail sketch of the main points of the gospel. It is these great truths which form the essentials of a quality teaching ministry within a local church. Of course, our curriculum should be the whole Bible, the whole counsel of God (Acts 20:27, AV). But we must major on explaining Christ and these truths surrounding his saving work from all the Scriptures (2 Timothy 3:15).

Being contemporary

In quality teaching the truths of Scripture will be stated and illustrated and applied to our hearers. In doing this we address the whole person. When we state the truth we address the mind. When we illustrate the truth we touch the imagination and emotions. When we apply the truth we address the will, and move people to action.

It is as we contemplate these three elements of preaching that we see most easily how to be contemporary and helpful to modern people. The great truths of the gospel which we have pointed out above can never change. It is anathema to change the message of Christ (Galatians 1:8–9). These are timeless truths which the Son of God shed his own blood to establish.

But the devil often hits back. He prejudices people against the eternal truth of God by parodying eternal facts as being simply 'old-fashioned and out of date'. However, as we think about stating the truths we find in Scripture and illustrating and applying them we see how, in the right sense, to be up to date.

State the truth

When a missionary goes to a foreign land he has to learn the language so that he can speak in the tongue that his hearers will understand. To people who lived fifty years ago our world would be a foreign country. So many things, including language, have changed. Preachers need to do their best to state the truths of the gospel accurately in modern language. Let me give an example. In my list of essential doctrines I have used the phrase 'penal substitution.' In many ways it is a great phrase. But most ordinary unchurched people would have difficulty in understanding it. Therefore, as we preach we will probably need to use other words which are more accessible to our modern hearers. It is essential that we make what is said in church intelligible to outsiders (1 Corinthians 14:22–25). Instead of saying that Jesus' death was a 'penal substitution', we might say that Jesus 'died in our place to take the punishment which our sin deserved'. Quality teaching will always seek to make Bible truth clearer to people rather than to obscure it with theological language.

Illustrate the truth

As we seek to encapsulate the truth in word pictures which engage our listeners' imaginations, once again we have the opportunity to plug the truth of God straight into today's world. We need to do our best to illustrate the truth by using stories and situations which link directly with contemporary life. For example, not long ago I heard about the wedding of a college girl. Much to the surprise of those attending the wedding, when it came to the part in the marriage ceremony when she had to say to the man about to become her husband 'and all my worldly goods I share with you,' she burst out laughing. The reason was that having just finished as a student all she had in the world was a debt of £6,000 owing from her student loan! How lovely that her bridegroom, knowing all about her debts, still married her and took on the debt as his own! But, of course, that is a simple illustration of what the Lord Jesus has done for each of us who believe. At the cross he claimed us as his bride, took our debt of sin upon himself and paid it in full. How Christ loves us!

Apply the truth

Many of the circumstances of life have changed since the Bible was written. The world has changed from being largely agricultural to being technological. Imperial thrones have fallen and we live in liberal democracies. Temptations come to us through many avenues, like TV and the internet, which our forebears knew nothing about. Such changes need to be recognized. For example, how are we to show Christian behaviour in driving our cars? When we have been 'cut up' by some other driver, we can certainly find a new application for the text, 'Do not repay anyone evil for evil' (Romans 12:17).

In such ways we stay true to the unchanging word of God yet give the lie to the devil's accusation that Christian faith is out of date.

God lives in his word

Our teaching can be done with variety—sometimes preaching from a passage, sometimes preaching from a single text, sometimes teaching on a topic and drawing together many passages and texts which relate to the subject. This teaching must be carried out prayerfully, guided by the Holy Spirit. It needs to be done with pace which holds the attention. It needs to be pursued in an unselfconscious way. Possibly the most helpful piece of advice I ever received as a young preacher was this: 'You are not called to be original, you are called to be helpful.' Perhaps you are in a little church which cannot afford its own pastor. You feel totally inadequate to the job of teaching the church and feeding the souls of the little fellowship with spiritual food. But if, with a humble heart, you would seek to do good to your brothers and sisters, you open your Bible and share with them whatever has helped you, be it from Bible commentaries or other Christian books, and you will not go far wrong.

One of the greatest preachers we have at present in our country confesses that he has hardly ever had an original thought in his life and that most of his sermons come from studying and putting the teachings from *Matthew Henry's Bible Commentary* into his own words. With such honest humility, this man has been of enormous help to multitudes of God's people. So let me encourage you, inadequate as you may feel, to 'feed the flock'.

As with humility and faith we open up God's Word something remarkable happens. God comes. Christ himself draws near. There are some remarkable New Testament texts which underline this, of which I now list three.

- *Romans 10:14*: 'How can they call on the one they have not believed in? And how can they believe in the one (of) whom they have not heard? And how can they hear without someone preaching to them?' I have put the word 'of' in brackets because the word is not in the original text. This implies that when in the Spirit a preacher declares the gospel, the congregation do not just hear about Christ, in a very real sense they hear Christ himself!

- *Ephesians 2:17*: 'He [Christ] came and preached peace to you who were far away and peace to those who were near. For through him we both have access to the Father by one Spirit.' Once again Paul is writing. This time it is to the Ephesian church. Those 'who were near' are the Jews. 'You who were far away' are the Gentiles. The Lord Jesus barely crossed over the borders of the Promised Land during his earthly lifetime, so how could he have come and preached peace to the Ephesians? The answer is that when the gospel is preached in Spirit and in truth, Christ himself is speaking. When the gospel was brought to Ephesus by Paul, Jesus was speaking through him.

- *1 Peter 2:2–3*: 'Like newborn babies, crave pure spiritual milk, so that by it you may grow up in your salvation, now that you have tasted that the Lord is good.' The phrase 'pure spiritual milk' is the Word of God. But notice what it is that Peter's readers taste through this pure spiritual milk. The Lord himself! Christ lives in his word. Of course, this is not the only place where the Lord lives. He lives in heaven. He lives among his people by his Spirit. But he does live in his Word.

So it is that when the Bible is humbly opened and explained with the purpose of glorifying God and feeding the souls of God's people Christ himself is known.

So it is that when we teach God's Word, we can do so with confidence and with authority, for God himself is in his Word. This is the most exciting encouragement to a church of any size. God himself lives in his Word and his Word will do the work. His Word will convert and encourage and direct and empower.

True worship

Many small churches become discouraged over the matter of worship. They see large congregations with music groups and gifted musicians. They hear modern worship songs which are full of encouragement and modern tempos. But all the small church has is perhaps a broken-down organ and some old hymn books. Now, personally, I enjoy many of the new Christian songs and the more modern instruments. But little church, these things are not of the essence of true worship. They are exciting and often moving, but they are not necessary for the true worship of God.

True worship is about living life for God with thankfulness from our hearts (Romans 12:1–2). And where the Word of God is taught and received gladly into believers' hearts resulting in faith in God and obedience to him, there is true worship (Psalm 95:6–8). If there is no heart love and obedience to Christ's word, then we can sing all the hymns (old or new) that we like, but we will just be drawing near to God with our lips while our hearts are far from him (Mark 7:6). It is vain 'worship'. This is why quality teaching is so important. Little church, your musical abilities may be meagre. But that is OK. God looks on the heart. Your old organ may be out of tune and your voices few and weak. But if your hearts are in tune with God and that shows through practical and thankful Christian living, then God is pleased. God receives your worship, offered in and through Christ Jesus, with great joy.

This is why quality teaching and our response to it is so important. Be encouraged. You can worship God just as well as any larger church.

7.
Quality hospitality

As students years ago, a group of us from the university Christian Union started attending a little Railway Mission church in the town where we were studying. We had passed the old chapel on our way to college each day and often wondered about it.

The reason we plucked up courage and eventually decided to try the church one Sunday was because although we had been attending a large Baptist church with good teaching, we felt anonymous. We felt we did not really know anyone there and no one knew us. We trooped in with the crowd each Sunday, enjoyed the teaching and then we trooped out. We longed for a more intimate and real Christian fellowship in church life as well as in the Christian Union.

The congregation in the Railway Mission was small. It consisted mostly of older people, with one or two youngsters from church families. In many ways it was excruciatingly old-fashioned for 'trendy' students like ourselves. But the warmth of the welcome and the openness and kindness of the hospitality shown to us there captured our hearts. We felt that we had entered a family, which gave something of a true reflection of the Lord's love for his children. We got to know older people and to learn from their spirituality. There was a very old railwayman there, who in his retirement spent many happy hours just copying out parts of the Bible into exercise books. 'I love the Word of God,' he would say, 'and writing it out helps me to take it in.' Then there was Annie. She had been born blind and was now very elderly and dependent on other people. But she was there in church every Sunday. She loved Christ and would say, 'I think of my blindness as a blessing. Sighted people have to see many horrible and sinful sights in this world. But the first thing I will ever see will be the face of my Lord Jesus when he calls me home.' These people opened their hearts and their homes to us and we learned so much.

The pastor of this church was a remarkable man. He was single and lived in two connected houses next to the chapel. He organized tea for students and anyone else who wanted to come each Sunday afternoon. The home was open. With space to spare it was not long before students in need of somewhere to stay were finding they could stay at the manse. Over the years this service to others developed especially among students from overseas. Foreign students are often more willing to hear about the gospel than people from our own country. A number of these folk from abroad became Christians. Young men from the Indian subcontinent,

Malaysia and beyond found a home in the pastor's house, and came under his Christian influence. From the hospitality of those days a Bible college started in Sri Lanka and continues to flourish. Also a number of men were led into the Christian ministry, both in this country and in the Far East.

This is the power of Christian hospitality. And small churches are able to offer hospitality just as much as larger churches. In many ways, true hospitality is easier for a small church. There can be a much more personal interest taken in people in a small group. Bigger churches tend to organize you as a group, whereas little churches know you as individuals.

The first church in Jerusalem was a very hospitable group. 'They broke bread in their homes and ate together with glad and sincere hearts, praising God ...' (Acts 2:46).

There are numerous commands in the New Testament exhorting us to be hospitable.

- 'Share with God's people who are in need. Practise hospitality' (Romans 12:13).

- 'Keep on loving each other as brothers. Do not forget to entertain strangers, for by so doing some people have entertained angels without knowing it' (Hebrews 13:1–2).

- 'Offer hospitality to one another without grumbling' (1 Peter 4:9).

These apostolic instructions apply first of all to caring for other Christians, but as we shall see they also apply to outsiders and those who do not yet belong to Christ.

Quality hospitality is the proper follow-through from a quality welcome and quality teaching. It shows that we are not just interested in people filling pews, but we are interested in people themselves for the Lord's sake.

The essence of hospitality

We can have wrong views of hospitality. In Scripture, it is not first of all about a loaded table. It is about an open door.

In our language we have the word 'xenophobia'. It means a fear or hatred of foreigners, and is associated with much that is sinful and racist. The New Testament word for hospitality is in many ways the opposite. It is the word 'philoxenia'. It is a composite of two words, 'phileo', a verb which means to love, and 'xenos', which means stranger. We remember the words of the Lord Jesus in the parable of the sheep and the goats. At the great judgement, part of the commendation which is given to the sheep by the great King says, 'I was a stranger and you invited me in' (Matthew 25:35). In primitive or lawless societies strangers were generally seen as enemies, because they were unknown. People were afraid of foreigners, so they were often shut out or driven away. The door was closed in their face. But Christ's people are meant to be different. We are meant to open our doors to new people. We can have them around for an hour or two and make them feel welcome. We may, as we are able and they have need, find ourselves asking them to stay with us for a longer time. That opening of our door speaks of a heart which is open to people.

So we need not be rich. We need not have a large house. We need not be great chefs or cooks. All we need is a door to open. It is when we feel the need to be impressive in our hospitality that it can become a burden. We can then easily forget (Hebrews 13:2), or start to grumble about it (1 Peter 4:9). There does not need to be the stress of making the house perfectly tidy, or of cooking a gourmet meal. This was the kind of attitude which got Martha into trouble when she was entertaining the Lord Jesus Christ (Luke 10:41–42). Of course, we should want people to be blessed by coming home with us, but we must not go to the extreme of turning it into a gala performance.

Obviously wisdom must be applied, but you do not have to be young or married to offer hospitality. When a church together has an open heart to outsiders, we can share the work. Then, though it may not be appropriate, for example, for a young single woman to invite a man back to her home when he visits the church, yet there will be someone else in the church who can do that and make him feel wanted and cared for and accepted.

- Hospitality speaks volumes for the gospel. As we have seen already, we live in a society which is becoming ever more individualistic. Many people are loners. Many people are divorced or come from broken homes. Many people have their own group of 'friends' but are closed to anyone from outside the group. In such a world it is refreshing and heart-warming to come across a group of Christian people with open hearts.

- Hospitality does involve giving time and effort to people. That means that we must give it some real priority in our lives. If our only priority is our own private comfort or not being disturbed as we see the next episode of our favourite TV programme, then it may well be that we never get around to offering hospitality. We will need to ask ourselves what is truly most important in our lives.

- Hospitality is a natural consequence of the gospel. In Scripture we find that as sinners we were foreigners to the holy God. We were lost. We were without God and without hope in the world. We were like wandering refugees with no place of refuge. We were 'alienated from God' because of our evil behaviour (Colossians 1:21). We were strangers to his ways, his covenant and his promises (Ephesians 2:12), and shut out of heaven because of our sin. But through his grace expressed in the blood of the Lord Jesus Christ, God opened the door to us and took us in. If God has done that for us, then we ought to do the same for others.

'Come and be with us for a while.' Christian hospitality is commanded of God's people.

The power of an open door

Let me just tell you Steve's story at this point to illustrate the power of hospitality in the hands of Christ.

Steve was born in West London into a large family. His father, who was from the Mediterranean, worked on the

Underground and his mother, from Ireland, insisted on the family attending mass at the local Catholic church.

Steve went to school in Fulham, but always felt he didn't fit in. He struggled to learn and did not enjoy good health. As a youngster he developed a drink and drugs problem. This led him towards truancy and he progressively became involved in shoplifting to fund his misuse of drugs and alcohol. He effectively left school at the age of thirteen taking a job as a tea-boy in a telephone shop.

His slide towards chronic alcoholism actually started when Steve was an altar boy at the age of eight. He would water down the communion wine to enable him to hide the neat remnant behind a cistern in the church toilet in order to drink it later in the day. Drinking made him feel warm, comfortable and excited. It helped him to escape from the difficulties he faced in life. An attempt at further education at a college just extended the cycle of drinking, drugs, fights and trips to hospital casualty departments.

By his early twenties Steve found himself living rough on the streets of London and getting work whenever he could. He frequently suffered fits as a consequence of his alcohol addiction and at twenty-five had his first stroke, resulting in his right hand being paralysed for a month. He had fears and anxieties and was often picked up by the police for violent behaviour. A cycle developed of being forced into detox programmes. He would come off the alcohol, only to leave and straightaway return to drinking. On reflection, Steve thinks he went around this loop about ten times. After a second stroke, at the age of thirty-five Steve reached rock bottom. In his own words, 'I ran out of options.' After three serious overdoses in as many days, he found himself once again in a London hospital casualty department.

From somewhere—and looking back now Steve believes the strength came from the Lord—he got on a train to Richmond where he had heard of a hostel. When he arrived, he was told there was no bed, but he was given an address in Leatherhead. He had no money, he was in pain, he hated everyone and he wanted to die. Everything seemed to depend on what would happen in Leatherhead. Desperate for a drink, he made it to the address. The door opened and he was welcomed by two Christians. They were a brother and sister who ran a shelter. They immediately said, 'Come in. Would you like a meal?'

Steve couldn't believe it. From the streets of London to a bed in Surrey—it seemed like a dream. He says, 'It was as if God had come down and slapped me round the head and said, "Wake up! This is different."'

They took Steve in, deloused him, burned his old clothes and gave him new ones. He slept in the hostel which was open from 6pm each night, and detoxed himself from alcohol in a hut on a nearby village green during the day. But this time it did feel different. This time it was going to be for good. He stayed off the drink. Steve was soon earning some pocket money doing a few jobs in the hostel and later he was introduced to the church to which the Christian brother and sister belonged. With the help of Alcoholics Anonymous and a good GP, Steve's life started to come back together. As he went along to church, he felt accepted, he felt he could be real, and as he listened week by week 'the gospel made loads of sense'. Praise God, it was not long before Steve came through to personal faith in Christ.

No doubt this lovely story has been repeated in the lives of others many times. But we must not miss the point. For Steve that open door of hospitality was a crucial turning point that led to him opening his heart to the Lord Jesus. Here is the power of Christian hospitality.

Spiritual importance

Not long ago in our own church, one of the elders carried out a survey. He sent a little questionnaire to church members who had been Christians for some time, or were brought up in a church. This elder has particular responsibility for our young people's fellowship and was thinking through priorities for the work. With this in mind he simply asked the adults what were their most lasting and positive memories of youth work in their church when they were young. There was one overwhelming answer which came through. The most lasting and spiritually positive memories from past experience of youth groups was to do with youth leaders spending time with small groups either taking them out somewhere or having the group back to their home. In other words, it was hospitality in its various different forms which impacted people for good. There was no collusion. People filled in the questionnaire quite independently.

Not only is hospitality spiritually important with respect to how it affects people, it is also spiritually important in what it represents in the eyes of God. It shows God that our faith is not just for Sundays. It shows the Lord that we do not want to box him into what happens 'at church' but we want him and his kingdom for all of life. We are not keeping God out of our homes. Sadly, there are some Christians who do like to try to restrict God to what happens in the chapel building on a Sunday. They set aside certain slots for God during Sunday and perhaps a mid-week evening, but they do not want to be disturbed outside those boundaries. This saddens the Lord. It is telling God, 'so far, but no further'. We are saying that to Christ, who did not say 'so far but no further', but went all the way to the cross for us. But when we open our homes, it is part of laying everything that we are and have at the Lord's feet. It is a very practical way of saying to the Lord, 'I and my family are totally at your disposal.'

There is a helpful illustration of repentance that is often used in explaining the gospel to people. It illustrates that although repentance marks the beginning of the Christian life, it is an ongoing process. We draw a plan view of a house, with the front door, the hallway, the sitting room, the kitchen, the bedroom etc. Becoming a Christian is like opening the front door of your life to the Holy Spirit. Once he has entered you truly belong to the Lord (Romans 8:14). When the Spirit of God enters he begins to work like a decorator who is renovating your inner life. He may begin by redecorating the hallway. But the Spirit wants to renew the whole of the interior of your house. As time goes on he wants to be given access to every room, and to keep those rooms up to scratch. He wants us to open every room of our lives. He does not want to find a sign on a door which bars him from entering any room. He wants to do a thorough job. Is our home life an area where God and his work are never really invited? Hospitality is a way of showing the Lord that our homes belong to him.

Your reaction?

What is your reaction to the down-and-outs or foreigners who from time to time turn up at church looking for help? The tramps are often sodden with drink and can be very damaged and demanding people. Frequently they are homeless or in need of food or a bath or a shave.

Our church policy is, if possible, never to give such people money. If we do, it may well be spent on drink and will do them more harm than good. However, we have ways of trying to help them practically, giving food or finding a night's accommodation for them, without involving money. But what is your reaction to such people? Do be careful how you treat the needy—even the 'undeserving' needy. We were needy and certainly 'undeserving' in our sin, but God treated us with kindness and saved us.

Do you remember the words of the Lord Jesus Christ in the great parable of the sheep and the goats? In the parable he pictures the final judgement with all the world standing before the great King. Then comes the momentous division between the sheep and the goats, between the saved and the lost. The saved are distinguished by having shown the marks of grace in their lifetime, while the lost have shown no such signs of grace. The marks of grace which identify those who belong to Christ involve us having tried to treat people the way God has treated us as Christians.

> Then the King will say to those on his right, 'Come, you who are blessed by my Father; take your inheritance, the kingdom prepared for you since the creation of the world. For I was hungry and you gave me something to eat ... I was a stranger and you invited me in.' Then the righteous will answer him, 'Lord, when did we see you hungry and feed you ... When did we see you a stranger and invite you in? ...' The King will reply, 'I tell you the truth, whatever you did for one of the least of these brothers of mine, you did for me'
>
> (Matthew 25:34–40).

Those strangers, those foreigners that come, may be Christians. Even those tramps and drunkards may yet become Christians and so be brothers of Christ. So be careful how you handle them. Your reaction to them will say something to God. Hospitality is spiritually important.

Follow up

Among the older people in our congregation a particular mid-week meeting that took place long before I came to the church seems to stand out in their memories. It seems to have marked something of a turning point in the life of the church. The previous pastor was taking the Thursday night Bible study and prayer meeting when he stopped and carefully asked the little group there the following serious question: 'If you were the Lord Jesus, and you had a new-born Christian, who like a tiny helpless baby needed looking after, would you send him or her to our church to be cared for?' The challenge seemed to shake a number of people there to their roots. I think there was bad feeling and tensions between people in the church at the time. People hung their heads. They had grown accustomed to thinking about what 'the church' should do for them, not about what they as the church should be doing for others. Ask yourself the question. Would the Lord send a new Christian to your church? Would 'baby Christian' find that people there had time for him? Would he find the church hospitable? Would he find spiritual acceptance and care?

Hospitality is very often the first step to effective follow-up. The new Christian needs teaching. He needs the pure milk of the word. He needs the Bible. That is the priority. But he is far more likely to be open and teachable if he finds that he is wanted and loved by the brothers and sisters. When we open the doors of our homes we are doing spiritual good.

Is there love in the fellowship which shows itself in giving time to people? Time, as has often been remarked, is the most precious commodity of all in today's busy world. Everyone seems to feel under pressure by the pace of modern life. If we can spend time on people, it indicates that they have a real place in our affections.

This is where those who are retired can come into their own. So often we think that the life of the church resides with the young people. But that is not true. Those who have finished their working lives, especially if they still have their health, are an immense resource. Perhaps in your little church the majority of people are getting on in years. They may not still have the energy they would like, but they have this most precious commodity—time.

The best piece of follow-up work I have ever seen was carried out by a dear retired couple in our congregation. A younger married couple were brought along to the church by the wife's recently converted brother. After a few weeks of them being in the congregation every Sunday night under the preaching of the gospel they put their faith in Christ. They were a couple with quite a history in worldly terms, which it is not necessary to go into. How were they to be grounded in Christ? How were they to be followed up? A retired couple, whose parents had been Christians and who themselves had a long pedigree of Christian life and church membership, were available. The couples were as different as chalk and cheese. The new converts were young, worldly wise, and switched on. The older couple came from dyed-in-the-wool church stock. How could it possibly work? But it did. Both couples really loved the Lord Jesus Christ, and the older couple would find time every week and spend hours with the young converts, delighting to talk through the things of God. A deep affection for each other sprang up across the generation gap and the cultural divide, and the new Christians were rooted and grounded in the Lord and went on to become great workers in his service. Genuine hospitality has so much in common with the sentiments of the apostle Paul when he writes, 'We loved you so much that we were delighted to share with you not only the gospel of God but our lives as well, because you had become so dear to us' (1 Thessalonians 2:8).

When ordinary church members open their homes and lovingly give of their time, springs of renewal start to flow in a church.

8.
Quality prayer

It is usually only possible to see turning points in the life of a church from a distance in retrospect. But as I look back, it is quite clear to me that many of the major steps forward in our own experience as a congregation are intimately connected with prayer.

In embarking upon ministry in the church my wife and I came to realize that one of the clear weaknesses with the church was that, by and large, it had lost connection with the people around the area in which the chapel is situated. As I have already indicated I think this is a continuing weakness in many churches. How was this to be remedied? How was the church to become a significant part of the community again and so bear witness for Christ? Ann and I had begun to pray about this quite seriously. We knew that unless we reconnected with ordinary people the church could not really be of much use to the Lord.

We ourselves had moved into the area around the church building and our children had begun to attend the local primary school. This seemed the right way forward in getting to know folk in the area. The school playground where mothers congregate to meet their youngsters at the end of the school day is a natural place to meet and to get acquainted with people. But then, as we prayed on, two things happened which stand out.

The first arose when Ann attended a school meeting for parents. At that meeting the headmistress announced that the school was looking for an extra parent-governor. It occurred to Ann that this might be a way to both serve the community and to get among people. However, she was concerned about whether it was the right thing. In the second chapter of the book of Nehemiah we come across that classic instance of the 'arrow prayer'. An 'arrow prayer' is the label we give to a silent prayer uttered in the heart on the spur of the moment as we are faced with a possible opportunity for Christ and his work. Nehemiah had been very saddened to hear of the walls of Jerusalem being broken down and the gates burned. As cup-bearer to the King of Persia he was meant to always show a smiling face. But the King noticed his sadness and enquired as to the reason for this. Nehemiah explained and the King asked him, 'What is it you want?' Here was an opportunity. But Persian kings were generally very unstable and explosive customers, and Nehemiah had no idea how his majesty would react if he told him what he would like to do. Nehemiah was put on the spot. We read Nehemiah's recollection of what happened next. 'Then I prayed to the God of heaven, and I answered the king ...' It was an 'arrow prayer', on the spur of the moment, which the Lord wonderfully answered. Nehemiah boldly asked the king to send him back to Jerusalem to rebuild it and the king said, 'Yes.'

As she sat in the school meeting with the possibility of becoming part of the school governing body before her, my wife sent a silent 'arrow prayer' to God. She prayed that although she hardly knew anyone at the meeting, since we had only recently moved to the area, if it were right in the Lord's sight for her to stand for election to the governors then someone else in the meeting would suggest her. It seemed very unlikely. But almost before her little prayer had finished she felt someone sitting behind her nudge her in the back. 'Why don't you become a governor? You would be good at that,' said Lesley, a mother of some friends of our children. Sure enough Ann became part of the governors. This was the start of a long involvement for her with the local school. This small prayer was to open many doors into the community.

'Fill the church!'

However, it is one thing for the pastor's wife to be part of the governing body of the school, it is another thing for local people to become acquainted with the church and for links to begin to form. The beginning of that second step very definitely came about once again through prayer.

This time the prayer came in the weekly prayer meeting. We met for prayer on Thursday evenings and concern for the locality of the church had begun to filter onto the agenda of members' prayers. With this on our minds one Thursday night one of the older, stalwart Christian ladies of the congregation, known for her prayer life, got up to pray in the prayer meeting. As she prayed she became very animated. She truly seemed to have taken hold of the Lord and it was as if she had a definite vision in her mind of what was required. She prayed clearly and distinctly that we would soon see the church building filled with people from the roads and houses around the chapel. Whether we had the faith we should have had to believe the prayer only the Lord knows. But certainly that prayer made an impact and stayed in our thoughts.

It should not have surprised us when the answer came, but it did. Out of the blue the headmistress contacted the church. There was a problem with the roof of the school hall. The harvest assembly to which all the parents of the school children are always invited was imminent. The hall was unusable. Would it be at all possible for the school to use our building for that assembly, and would the pastor like to give a five-minute talk about harvest to the children and parents? Of course we said, 'Yes.' The prayer from the prayer meeting was wonderfully answered. The forbidding wooden doors of our old chapel must have put off many a passer-by over the years, but now those doors were wide open, and mums and dads and grandmas and aunties and whoever were filing into a church building which otherwise they would never have thought of entering!

It was not long before the school realized that it was much easier to hold all their big annual assemblies in our building.

For many years harvest, Christmas and Easter time saw the children and their families gathering within the chapel walls. Real connections were formed. Whether we always made the best of the possibilities the Lord opened up in this way I do not know. But certainly a good solid children's work on a week-night evening, made up mostly of youngsters from the locality, began to flourish and in God's goodness has flourished ever since. But the lesson is that the turning points had been firmly rooted in prayer.

Small church prayer

Jesus makes it crystal clear that prayer is something which small churches can do just as well as larger churches. In many a small gathering his words have brought encouragement. 'I tell you that if two of you on earth agree about anything you ask for, it will be done for you by my Father in heaven. For where two or three come together in my name, there am I with them' (Matthew 18:19–20).

What Jesus says has two parts. There is the promise, and then there is the reason why the promise is true. The promise is that what the people of God agree to ask the Father will be done. It needs to be noted that this 'agreement' is mentioned in the context of a passage in the New Testament on 'church discipline'. It insists on our keeping good relationships in the church and clearing up any sin there may be between us (Matthew 18:15–17). The reason their prayer will be answered is that the Lord Jesus, God's Son and our Saviour, is among such a group of Christians and one with them when they ask the Father. The Father always hears and answers his Son's requests (John 11:41–42).

Notice what, according to the Lord Jesus, God answering the prayers of the church both *does not,* and *does,* depend on.

It *does not* depend upon the number of people praying. Jesus says that even two or three people in Christ, meeting in love and agreement with each other, will see their prayers answered. This should not be taken as an argument to neglect attending the church prayer meeting: 'O, as long as there are two or three people there, that will be good enough.' What Jesus is saying means that small groups should not be discouraged, not that we should use this as an excuse for spiritual laziness.

It *does* depend upon the unity and agreement of the group. It depends on people in the church repenting when they offend others and forgiving one another those offences. It depends on keeping short accounts with regard to relationships in churches. It depends on the reality of Christian love in the church. This sadly is something which British Christians are not very good at and it leads to a lack of power in the prayer meeting.

When there are tensions and offences we tend to try to deal with them in a middle-class 'English' kind of way, pretending that nothing has happened. We keep quiet and say nothing, while often the hurts and jealousies continue to boil beneath the surface. This is disastrous with respect to church prayer. The title of this chapter is 'quality prayer'. Quality prayer depends on quality relationships. This is emphasized repeatedly in the New Testament (Matthew 5:23–24; Matthew 6:9–14; 1 Peter 3:7 etc.). The reason why so many church prayer times lack the required quality is that we do not pay sufficient attention to keeping the loving oneness of the church.

However, it is worth picking up on another encouragement here for the small church. It is not always true, but usually it is easier for a smaller church to attain and maintain the kind of love and unity among the brothers and sisters that the Lord wants to see. With fewer people there are fewer relationships that can go wrong. With fewer people it is harder to maintain the pretence that 'everything is OK' when it is not. With fewer numbers to watch over, the elders and leaders can be more closely involved in seeking to bring about reconciliation in the body of Christ. Where a little church can generate a real team spirit among its members that team spirit is usually harder to break.

The church on its knees

We all agree that the church generally is going through a lean and difficult time in the Western world at present. We live in days when it is hard to get a hearing for the gospel. It is true that the materialistic, consumer society does have a strong hold over the average person and leads them to dismiss the claims of Christ almost before they are presented. The prevalence of these attitudes in times of prosperity should not surprise us. Right back in the time of Moses God warned his own people Israel that wealth and ease would lead even them into the temptation to forget God (Deuteronomy

8:10–14). Again in Jesus' parable it was the *rich* fool who had no thought for God (Luke 12:16–21). So we should not be nonplussed by the situation we face. It is actually very predictable.

But however we want to couch the hardness of the society around us to the gospel, the bottom line is that it is a spiritual problem. It comes back to satanic activity. Whatever he is using as his means, be it materialism or anything else, 'The god of this age has blinded the minds of unbelievers, so that they cannot see the light of the gospel of the glory of Christ' (2 Corinthians 4:4). We have to realize that in Satan we are up against a mighty and devious foe. Therefore, it is not new methods or clever sermon titles or even building bridges with non-Christians that is going to change anything. Ultimately it is only the almighty power of God which can break the chains and take the blindfolds from people's eyes. The church needs the power of God and all Scripture asserts that the power of God comes by prayer. When the church is beaten to its knees it needs to be on its knees in prayer!

The pattern for prayer

How are we to pray together? It is worth noting that the great pattern prayer Jesus gave, which we usually call 'The Lord's Prayer', is a corporate prayer. It was given in response to Jesus' disciples as a group asking him, 'Lord, teach us to pray' (Luke 11:1). Its phraseology is all in terms of the plural 'us' not the singular 'me'. So it is right to let the Lord's Prayer set the agenda for the church prayer meeting. Most importantly, we need to come to God humbly as our majestic Father, with a loving attitude towards others, trusting in the name of our Saviour, the Lord Jesus Christ.

The Lord's Prayer contains expressions of worship ('hallowed be your name'); concern for Christ's return, obedience and world mission ('your kingdom come. May your will be done on earth as it is in heaven'); requests for daily needs and forgiveness ('give us this day our daily bread. Forgive us our sins'); requests for protection from Satan, the world and our sinful selves ('lead us not into temptation but deliver us from the evil one').

These then are the topics that ought to shape our prayer times together. Many a time I have found that we have had to refocus on these matters. It is so easy for the church prayer meeting to become taken over by concerns for illnesses, redundancies and personal needs among the members that the rest get forgotten. While indeed we must love and care for each other, we must centre our prayer meetings first of all on God himself—his glory and the coming of his kingdom. We must not let one item on the agenda take over and dominate proceedings. It makes our prayer times monstrously misshapen. It is antithetical to quality prayer. By using the Lord's Prayer as our template we are letting the Lord Jesus set the agenda.

In particular we should take seriously that the Lord's Prayer begins with worship. There are many words in the New Testament concerning worship which overlap with each other—praise, blessing, thanksgiving etc. The apostle Paul often presses upon us the need to be thankful as we approach

God (Philippians 4:6–7; Ephesians 5:20; 1 Thessalonians 5:18). In order to counteract that self-centred tendency to let our troubles and sicknesses mushroom and take over the prayer meeting, it might be good to get into the habit of always beginning with a time of worship. 'Counting our blessings', especially the blessings of salvation, makes it simple to move into worship and thanksgiving.

Worship and thanksgiving encapsulate the proper attitude of the creature to our Creator, and of the sinner to our Saviour. Worship is the atmosphere of heaven where even the sinless angels continually adore and praise their King. A quality prayer meeting will always have an element of that same atmosphere.

Practicalities

The great need for any church, big or small, is the power of God. This comes through the prayer of people who are truly surrendered to Christ. How can a small church improve its praying? Here are a few practical suggestions.

- Many people are under great pressure from their work and do not get home until well into the evening. By the time they have got home and had a meal it is difficult to make it to the prayer meeting. Why not provide a simple supper at the beginning of the evening? Then people could come straight to church from the train, eat together and then join the prayer time.

- Unless there are exceptional circumstances keep strictly to time with respect to ending the prayer meeting. If people have come to church from an exhausting day at the office it is wrong to expect too much of them. Keeping to time will respect their need to get some relaxation and rest, and hopefully encourage them to come to pray regularly.

- Make sure that the lion's share of the time is given to prayer. If there is a Bible study, keep it to a minimum. There is plenty of time for preaching and teaching on Sundays. If you spend time flagging up topics for prayer, again keep it slick and short in order to leave time to pray. It might be good to use an overhead projector with topics already written up when people arrive.

- If informing the prayer meeting about different areas of church concern are shared among different members of the church that can help to keep things moving. Rather than just relying on the pastor (who perhaps is already burdened) to provide the information this can be a shared work and so give the church as a whole more of a feeling of ownership of the prayer meeting. Who will tell us how outreach is going? Who will keep us informed about the persecuted church? Missionary interest?

- It is no good denying that sometimes prayer is hard work. It is part of a spiritual warfare. Sometimes it has to be a struggle, a wrestling, in order for the victory to be won (Colossians 4:12), but if we do all we can to fan into flame that spirit of thankfulness in the prayer meeting we will also find that it becomes a spiritually refreshing time. If we can tap into this spring of refreshment then it will encourage Christians to come again and again to pray.

There is much more that can be said. Getting the men of the church to pray together in prayer triplets not only increases prayer, but provides a great source of close fellowship. Many churches find it helpful to have a week of prayer once or twice a year. How about a night or a half-night of prayer? There is something symbolic and encouraging in praying through the darkness of the night until the first rays of dawn begin to break. Such prayer may well be the means of bringing a new day spiritually to an embattled church.

Who knows what may be the consequences when just a few people meet regularly for prayer? Back at the beginning of the nineteenth century a group of like-minded students in Massachusetts used to meet in a grove near their campus for prayer and discussion about God's work. One day during their time of prayer they were caught in a violent thunderstorm and took refuge in a nearby haystack. There they prayed on! Somehow it turned into the most intense time of prayer. Church history now recognizes that it was out of this time of prayer that emerged the American Board of Commissioners for Foreign Missions, which was the beginning of the great tide of missionary work that has swept around the world from America.

Who knows what a small, committed prayer meeting can accomplish? Who knows where God will lead when just a few of his people seek him earnestly in prayer? We should not be surprised that small prayers can lead to great things, for Scripture assures us that we have a great God who is able to 'do immeasurably more than all we ask or imagine, according to his power that is at work within us' (Ephesians 3:20).

9.
Fighting discouragement in a small church

The truth is that God can and does use small churches. If we were to ask, 'Where was Spurgeon converted?' the answer is, 'In a small church.' The greatest preacher of the nineteenth century came to Christ in very humble circumstances. He was converted on a snowy day in Colchester, in a Primitive Methodist chapel. His autobiography tells us, 'In that chapel there may have been a dozen or fifteen people.' Yet as he heard the 'stupid' preacher expound on Isaiah's words, 'Look unto me and be ye saved, all the ends of the earth,' young Charles Spurgeon was saved. What a wonderful worldwide ministry flowed from that little service! What seemed an insignificant meeting in the world's eyes turned out to be of incalculable importance. And did that little Methodist church know what had been accomplished among them on that day as they went home? Yet God had used them.

There is nothing wrong with being a small church. God uses the little flock just as much as the massive congregation. But, of course, in the kind of world we live in, with its emphasis on size, it is not always easy to remain hopeful and cheerful when we are few in numbers.

How do we fight discouragement in a small church? That is the question to which we now turn.

Key players

I want to suggest to you that the key people in fighting discouragement in a small church are the leadership. If the leaders are men who can, without pretence, sustain an optimistic, hopeful outlook, supported by each other (even of two or three), then the church, though small, can rejoice in its assets. It can be a place of love and joy. But if the leadership is gloomy and always sees the cup as half-empty rather than half-full, then that spirit can bring down the church.

I was talking with a pastor of a little congregation at a Christian conference not long ago, and thinking about the future of the church, and the next generation of leaders. He said that he had been greatly encouraged by a young man in his congregation who was godly, gifted and a fine preacher. As the minister was moving towards retirement, in a subtle way he asked the young man about what his thoughts were for the future: 'Any possibility of entering the ministry?' The young man's reply was blunt and startling: 'A life of poverty and a continual battle with depression is not for me!'

From his observation of churches and ministers that was the young man's candid conclusion. If you are a pastor, I have to tell you, you (and I) have got to stop complaining. We have got to crack this problem of discouragement which we all face. Not only is it unhelpful to us, it is unhelpful to the churches. Indeed, if we are not careful we are going to rob the future church of its leaders! So this chapter is really for leaders of the church. But I hope that ordinary church members will not skip it. If you read on, it may well help you to be a better encourager in the church too—not least to the leaders!

If it is true that the pastor/leaders hold the key to fighting discouragement in the church, then our question has somewhat changed. It now becomes, 'How does God help a man who faces a difficult and discouraging ministry?' This is an important subject. In trying to answer it, we will find it profitable to look at the call of the prophet Isaiah. Why Isaiah? Because, if you know your Bible you will remember that right from the beginning, God told the prophet that (in numerical terms) his ministry was going to be a failure. The people of Israel would close their ears against Isaiah's message (Isaiah 6:10). They would not repent. The people to whom Isaiah prophesied were going to be judged. They would be cut down. There would be just a stump of the tree left. It is a sobering prospect for a man who has just received the call of God.

Therefore we can ask the question, 'How did the LORD prepare his servant for that?' We will spend a little time looking at Isaiah 6, which records the famous call of the prophet. It would be good to read through that chapter of the Bible before we go any further. We will consider it under three headings: the causes, consequences and cure of discouragement.

The causes of discouragement

Some discouragements are peculiar to small churches, but we need to see an overall picture.

Generally

A blind gorilla who was bullied by her fellow inmates at Bristol Zoo has had her sight restored by an NHS eye surgeon who performed a cataract operation on her. Romina's recovery came as a shock to her previous tormentors, when she chased off another gorilla who used to steal her food. The surgeon who performed the operation was Jenny Watts of the Royal Hampshire Hospital: 'She was almost like a human patient,' she told *The Times*, 'apart from the pungent smell.'

You get those kinds of silly stories in news magazines under such headings as, 'It wasn't all bad.' Similarly, the old 'and finally' stories on ITV's *News at 10* used to be of a more light-hearted type. Such snippets are fairly innocuous. They mean very little. But their function is to try to cheer people up. And the reason is that the world we live in is a naturally discouraging place. Even at the best of times, there is not much good news. Of course! Christian, we live in a fallen world which is at odds with its Maker. We live in a world where sin has marred everything. So to be called like Isaiah to be a servant of God, urging people to repentance, is bound to involve opposition and conflict. We should expect to have to battle with discouragement. It is not something exclusive to your little church.

I was always struck reading the words of Thomas Hayward, the bishop's chaplain, examining John Wesley for holy orders: 'Do you know what you are about? You are bidding defiance to all mankind. He that would live a Christian priest ought to know that, whether his hand be against every man or no, he must expect that every man's hand should be against him.'

Even as a shepherd and helper of God's people, you are going to be exposed to the rough edge of life. You are going to be involved most often with people in various forms of trouble. If you pastor a bigger church you will see even more problems! There are more sinners, with more troubles! So discouraging circumstances are generally our lot in a fallen world. It is a heresy to teach otherwise.

Specifically

Let us highlight some of the specific discouragements Isaiah faced.

• *The frailty and failure of Christian leaders.* King Uzziah (v. 1) had been a godly king, but in pride had sinned grievously. He had overstepped the mark trying to burn incense in the temple and become priest as well as king. So God struck him with leprosy. From then on he was a recluse until he died (2 Chronicles 26:16–21).

   How discouraging it is when powerful ministries (which once encouraged us) are toppled by sin? We can think of many friends and even role models who have become casualties in the spiritual battle. They are now out of the Christian ministry.

- *The despising of God and his name.* The seraphs extol God (v. 3) as the Holy One. But Isaiah lived at a time when God seemed far away and people mocked 'the Holy One of Israel' (see Isaiah 5:19–20). He lived among a people of unclean lips (6:5). We live in a culture where evil is called good and good is called evil. Christians are in a despised minority in our land. We feel rejected and unwanted by society around us. And somehow we are even more sensitive to that in a small church.

- *The awareness of our own sins.* That can be so discouraging. Isaiah certainly was made to feel his own inconsistency and hypocrisy. 'Woe to me!' he cried. 'I am a man of unclean lips' (v. 5). The devil comes and accuses us: 'How can you preach to people or lead them, when you are such a sinner?' Then he adds: 'No wonder God cannot bless your ministry!' We feel like giving up.

- *The sight of decline in the churches.* Isaiah was called to serve through a period of dreadful deterioration (vv. 11–12). He will speak for God, 'until the cities lie ruined and without inhabitant, until the houses are left deserted and the fields ruined.' We see spiritual desolation all around us. We see it in the smallness of our congregation. We fear other people blame us. 'If only we had a better preacher!' We feel desperately demoralized. And in a small church there are so few with whom to share the work.

- *The unacceptability of our message.* Look at what Isaiah

had to declare: 'Be ever hearing but never understanding; be ever seeing, but never perceiving' (vv. 9–10). He was indicting people for their sins and sinful blindness to God. 'How unkind,' the self-congratulating world might say. It was a message of severe judgement. We too have to tell people they are such sinners. We too have to try to make them see that left to themselves they are unable to turn to God, and need his grace. We too in a multi-faith, pluralistic society, have to preach that there is only one way of salvation that is found in the love of God in Jesus Christ. We are right out of step with our culture. This is tough.

Other factors

On top of those we have mentioned there are other factors. We are not all the same. Church leaders have different temperaments, personality types and body chemistry. Isaiah, Jeremiah and Ezekiel were very different men. Do we know ourselves? Some of us are more resilient to trouble and others of us are not. Some of us tend towards introversion and melancholy. Dr Lloyd-Jones writes, 'If one is born with the temperament that tends towards the more serious, despondent type, then the devil is likely to take full advantage of that fact.'[1]

Then there is often the problem of poverty, insufficient finance. Sadly, so often churches expect ministers and their families to survive on less than other people. This can get us down.

So we can see that discouragement has many causes.

The consequences of discouragement

Generally speaking, discouragement leads to varying degrees of misery and paralysis and uselessness. If this affects the leadership, soon it will affect the whole church.

We can try to summarize briefly the consequences for the pastor under three headings.

a. Christian service

Isaiah was called to serve (v. 8). 'Whom shall I send?' asks the Lord. Isaiah eagerly replies, 'Here am I. Send me!' And the Lord says 'Go.' When we are discouraged we pull back from the service of God. We do not volunteer like Isaiah. We feel there is no point, especially if the church is small. Our prayers dry up. We may even pull out from service completely. We may quit the ministry.

Isaiah was called to 'go' (v. 9). When we are discouraged, we no longer go out with the gospel, we may even give up on evangelism.

Isaiah was given his message (vv. 10–11). It was a difficult message. It was not one which would readily gain popular approval. When we are discouraged, we no longer set forth the truth plainly. Rather we may be tempted to change our gospel message in order to curry favour with people. In 2 Corinthians 4:1 Paul speaks of not losing heart. But he sees that the consequences of losing heart can be adopting 'secret and shameful ways, using deception and distorting the word of God' (2 Corinthians 4:2).

b. Personal life

Discouraged people feel bad. They feel trapped in the darkness. If we do not handle the discouragement in a godly way we are exposing ourselves to dire consequences.

Bitterness. Some hardy souls stoically carry on with their Christian lives, but they become bitter, acrimonious people. Secretly they are blaming God and other people. Rather than adorning the doctrine of grace with gracious lives, their bitter spirit puts outsiders off the gospel!

Depression. Some dear people snap under the pressure. They burn out. They may fall into clinical depression and need medical help. We find even some of the greatest characters of Scripture overwhelmed by trouble, with morbid or suicidal thoughts (1 Kings 19:4).

Adultery. Recently I listened to a familiar sad tale from a man who is now out of the ministry. Adultery is never excusable, but the pattern is so familiar. 'I was discouraged and feeling worthless. No one at church encouraged me. My wife gave me little comfort, and then along came Angela, and I just thought "Why not, there's no joy anywhere else!"' And of course, it is not just adultery but other kinds of sin that arise in a similar way.

Hypocrisy. When discouragement comes and a church leader reacts by turning to the world to taste of its 'pleasures', very often he will seek to hide it from others. He will be one thing at church and a completely different person in private. He may well develop a hidden life. This is hypocrisy.

Church member, you need to help your pastor. You need to look out for him. He is often Satan's prime target. Encourage him.

c. Church life

If the devil can bring leaders into such a disheartened state, he knows that it will generally discourage the whole church. He knows that a discouraged church easily becomes a disunited and unhappy church, with people blaming each other for the fact that things are not so good. And when a church is disunited, people can start to depart, to jump ship. It is not long before we find that a disunited church becomes a dwindling church. That makes people even more discouraged and so speeds the downward spiral.

There is nothing wrong with being a small church, but beware of becoming a discouraged small church. A discouraged church often eventually turns into a non-existent church.

That is why the devil is so careful and attentive to pick up on every piece of disheartening ammunition he can find, and turn it into a fiery dart of discouragement against leaders. No wonder the New Testament is so full of commands to love one another and encourage each other.

The cure of discouragement

Let me here particularly address the church officers. I am thinking of other elders and the deacons. These are the folk who are often around the pastor. You can see that a discouraged pastor is bad news for everyone. To you church officers, therefore, I have to say that you will probably have a discouraged pastor unless you encourage him. How?

There are three key areas of encouragement.

- *Prayer.* The battle is spiritual. This is the first priority. The apostle Paul asked often for other people to pray for him (Ephesians 6:19; Colossians 4:3). If the apostle Paul needed people to pray for him, do you think your pastor doesn't?

- *Finance.* I remember an article R. T. Kendall had written for *Evangelical Times* some years ago. It was entitled 'Why we have such poor preachers', and one of the main thrusts of his article went along the following lines.

> How can you expect a man to concentrate on prayer and preparing a fine sermon when he is worried that he cannot pay his bills? How can he give himself for the good of the church when he is worried that he has no real pension? How can he concentrate on the ministry when lurking at the back of his mind is the fact that he will have no house of his own for the future? In this whole area I have to congratulate my own flock. When I began as a young pastor the church decided that generally speaking my salary would be the average of the other elders' salaries from their secular employment. I was neither richer nor poorer. It was a good decision and God blessed the church. After all, the salary we pay our minister is a practical reflection of how valuable we see the Word of God to be in the church.

- *Verbal encouragement.* Have you or your family benefited from the ministry of the preacher? Then tell him so. And tell others in the church too. Don't flatter the man, but whenever there is legitimate cause to thank God for the ministry then why not verbalize it? As we read the epistles how often Paul tells the churches when he is encouraged by them! Encouraging the pastor and telling others can warm the atmosphere of a congregation.

Now let me address the pastors. How did the LORD seek to prepare Isaiah against losing heart? How was Isaiah inoculated against discouragement? I believe that inoculation was part and parcel of the great vision of God by which the Lord called his servant into the ministry. I believe that this cure for discouragement applies just as much today. I believe this cure applies to people in small churches as well as in large. This vision of God is surely the key. Let us consider what Isaiah saw.

The holiness of God

The great theme of Isaiah is the holiness of God. The LORD is so vast, even the hem of his robe fills the temple (v. 1). He is so awesome that although his seraphic attendants are described, there is no description of the LORD himself. He is too holy. The angels around God's throne are no bored time-servers, looking to end their shift of the repetitive praise of God. They are absolutely enraptured and enthralled (v. 3). 'Holy, holy, holy is the LORD Almighty; the whole earth is full of his glory.'

God's holiness refers not only to his absolute moral purity, but also to his transcendence, his complete 'otherness'. God's whole way of existence, his whole mode of being, is different and separate from ours. We are created; he is the great uncreated. We are dependent; he is utterly self-contained and self-sufficient. The vision of God's holiness changed Isaiah's life. Pastor, you serve *this* God. He is the audience of your ministry.

Our church supports a little church in a nearby village. The pastor there is one of our members. The church is tucked away, right out of sight. It was very small, on the verge of closing. But since he went there it has begun gradually to pick up. Why? He is unstinting in his door-to-door ministry. There are just a few to help him. But one Saturday morning every month, out they go, even though the reception is often poor. Why carry on? 'Because God has called us to it,' is his answer. He is an example to us all of perseverance. What the results are, what other people think of us is of no consequence. He has an audience of one. That one is the all-holy God. For us, the fear of man is the cause of so much discouragement. That will only ever be cured by the true fear of God.

The grace of God

Isaiah, feeling mortified by his sins, cried out, 'Woe to me!' We can identify with that, can't we?

For introspective, serious Christians, the awareness of our own sins is a source of great discouragement. We can be so overcome by the sight of our guilt and our evil hearts that we can wonder, 'Am I a Christian at all?'

But as Isaiah agonizes over his guilt, at the bidding of God (it can be for no other reason), one of the seraphs leaves his rapturous duty of worshipping God and 'with a live coal in his hand, which he had taken with tongs from the altar' he touched Isaiah's mouth and said, 'See, this has touched your lips; your guilt is taken away' (vv. 6–7). The altar in the temple from which the burning coal is taken symbolizes the entire provision of sacrifice. The great sacrificial system God had instituted in the temple was for the sins of his people. God loves sinners. As the seraph touches him Isaiah is totally cleansed and made fit for God. This is not by his own efforts but by God's free grace. 'Your sin is atoned for,' says the angelic messenger (v. 7). Pastor, that goes for you too.

Dr Lloyd-Jones writes for the sensitive Christian, so aware of their own failings, 'The devil says, "Look at your record, there is only one conclusion to draw, you have never been a Christian." Answer the devil by telling him that what makes a man a Christian is not anything he finds in himself (good or bad), it is "Jesus' blood and righteousness". Thank God for this, for if we all examined ourselves truly and tried to decide on the basis of one's own life's record whether we are Christians or not, there would not be a single Christian! There is only one thing that makes a Christian—His righteousness—nothing else.'[2]

The call of God

Isaiah now hears the call of this transcendent, enthralling, gracious God (v. 8). And he does what anybody would do in such a situation. He forgot all about himself, and offered his life without reserve to the LORD. What a privilege to serve *him*. Isaiah laid down his life.

How many of our discouragements are anchored in an illegitimate preoccupation with ourselves. We are concerned with '*my* ministry', '*my* ambitions', '*my* feelings', '*my* reputation', '*my* security', '*my* ...' When a heart is being filled with the greatness of God and his service, there is less room for questions like, 'What are people going to think of me or do to me?' Such an attitude avoids so many pitfalls which lead to discouragement.

The glory of God

Part and parcel of Isaiah's vision was that he saw into heaven, the home of God. He tasted the reality of the perfect world beyond this one. He had seen the glory. The apostle Paul said, 'I consider that our present sufferings are not worth comparing with the glory that will be revealed in us' (Romans 8:18).

He also wrote, 'Therefore we do not lose heart. Though outwardly we are wasting away, yet inwardly we are being renewed day by day. For our light and momentary troubles are achieving for us an eternal glory that far outweighs them all' (2 Corinthians 4:16–17).

Notice, the troubles can work for us, achieve for us, a weight of glory! No wonder the New Testament church learned, not to be discouraged by trouble, but to welcome it (James 1:2). Paul boasted in his sufferings. Isaiah longed for one thing, to go through all the difficulties, and to arrive before God's throne of glory to hear the words, 'Well done.' When you are discouraged, fix your eyes on God's 'Well done.'

The Son of God

Here we have something of an advantage on Isaiah. The great prophet saw the awesome Lord sitting on the throne. In that wonderful chapter 53 he also foresaw the servant of the Lord, who would be pierced for our transgressions and crushed for our iniquities (53:5). But did he realize it was the same person?

Yet of course, John's Gospel tells us that it was. Quoting from Isaiah 6, John 12:40–41 states that it was Jesus whom Isaiah saw. Doesn't the fact that we are loved so much, by such a person, put all our discouragements into a rather different perspective?

In the light of all this we need to draw a sharp conclusion. Can't we see that complaining is a sin? Can't we see why the whole tenor of the New Testament is that we are commanded to celebrate? 'Rejoice in the Lord always. I will say it again: Rejoice!'

'But you do not understand', says someone. 'It is because I love the Lord that I find it so hard to see his cause dwindling, and his name despised. That's why I get so discouraged.' Very well. There are some legitimate sentiments there for all of us. But that forgets the last element of Isaiah's vision, which is in fact central to it all. Isaiah saw God who is truly God.

The sovereignty of God

He saw the Lord upon a throne (v. 1), higher than all other thrones. An earthly king had died but he saw the King whose throne is for ever, and therefore whose plans are able to outrun, outlast and outplay all other plans. Isaiah is overcome because 'My eyes have seen the King, the LORD Almighty' (v. 5).

Yes, our days are days of small things. Yes, there is much to disturb us. But these things are in his hands. And just as with the Assyrian invasion which ruined Israel, and later the Babylonian exile which devastated Judah, ultimately these things were the darkness against which the glory of the Lord shone more brightly. In just the same way, the present darkness of our land will only serve to make the Lord more glorious when he comes either in reviving power, or to the great consternation of the ungodly at the Parousia, the Second Coming.

An old hymn by Thomas Moore contains the line: 'Earth has no sorrow that He cannot cure.'[3] As we look to the God of heaven we will even be able to overcome the giant of discouragement which so often attacks us.

Notes

1. *Christian Warfare,* D. Martyn Lloyd-Jones, Banner of Truth, p.303.

2. *Christian Warfare*, p.306.

3. From the hymn 'Come, ye disconsolate, where're ye languish' by Thomas Moore, the Irish poet. No. 575 in the Baptist Church Hymnal (Revised) of 1933.

10.
The resources of heaven

The Sudan Interior Mission had sent into the land of Ethiopia trained missionaries who had worked hard during the 1920s and 1930s. After nine years of intense outreach and effort they had assembled just forty-eight converts to Christ.

Then Mussolini's Italian army invaded and the missionaries had to go. Leaving their place of work behind they were very concerned about the little group of believers alone in that vast land. What would happen to them? How could they possibly survive? But when the missionaries returned after the war was over, they were astonished. The church in Ethiopia now numbered 12,000 souls! During those few years God had been mightily at work through those few young, inexperienced and 'unprofessional' believers. We must not let our slim resources put us off doing what needs to be done for the Lord. God is able to work whatever the circumstances.

Small is beautiful

This chapter is about accessing the resources that God has for his people. But before we get to that, I want first to underline some more reasons why small churches can be thankful, and not be discouraged by their smallness. Already we have touched on some. We have mentioned that generally larger churches have more pastoral problems simply because there are more people. We have mentioned that a smaller fellowship has potential for a greater depth of fellowship among the whole congregation, simply because there are less people. We have mentioned that when God begins to use a small congregation it is plain that he is providing the power. He receives the glory. Therefore small is beautiful. But there are more reasons not to be too downcast about being a small group.

Institutionalization

The first is that large, long-established churches do tend to suffer from the problem of 'institutionalization'. Over the years, many social scientists have pointed out this phenomenon to which all organizations, including local churches, are prone. There is a pattern of rise and fall, which works in the following way.

A new work is born amid excitement and enthusiasm. This is the *initiation* of the work. At this stage the organization is relatively formless and its attitudes flexible. Then comes a period of *consolidation* during which a leadership pulls things together giving more structure to the work. Next it enters a period of maturity and maximum efficiency and stability.

But then it becomes a victim of its own success. There is no need for new ideas; everything is running well. So there often follows *fossilization*. A self-perpetuating bureaucracy develops, and it becomes insensitive to changing needs. Spontaneity is lost. Commitment becomes half-hearted. This then leads into a period of *disintegration*. That sadly is the story of many churches. Perhaps the small congregation you are in is the remains of a church at the end of such a cycle. But do not be too downcast. In fact, being at the end of such a cycle can be a blessing in disguise. It could be that you are now in a position to start afresh; and that is exciting. You see, while a church still has numbers but is actually fossilizing it will still hope that it does not need to change. It will still hope that radical surgery is not required. But having got to rock bottom, a church is then in a position to put the past behind and start again from scratch. To illustrate, take the example of reconstructing a chapel building. If the old structure is still in place there is a big demolition work to be done before the rebuild can begin. But if the old structure has already fallen, if it has already been razed to the ground, then it is far simpler to start the rebuild. In the same way, a small church can look upon itself as God having cleared the ground ready for a fresh start.

Large churches which are actually small churches

The second reason why a small church can be thankful for its smallness is because of its compactness. Let me explain. I have often noticed a rather disturbing situation. It seems to me that many larger churches are actually small churches, but with a very large fringe. In so many larger churches it is a small group of dedicated folk who do the majority of the work. These dear folk are stalwarts for Christ. They give themselves unstintingly to the work. But if they ask for help in manning the Sunday school or the coffee rota, or whatever, there are no volunteers. There are just a few workers and they have to carry all the rest who are just passengers. The majority joined the church in order to be part of a 'successful' congregation, but at the same time to lose themselves and be anonymous among the hundreds who attend. They do not want to join the workers. What a desperate situation that is. But, by contrast, usually in a small church those who attend are those who are prepared to work. It is a compact group, a band of brothers and sisters who, though they are small in number, know that they can rely on each other to help out if they possibly can. It is not easy being a small church. But it is even less easy being a large church which is actually a small church. So thank God for being a small church.

Relying on the Lord

It is true that when churches become bigger there is a tendency to drift into self-reliance. The old question, which many preachers have asked of congregations over the years, is still relevant today, but especially to big churches. 'If Jesus was to withdraw his presence from your church what would change?' For many larger churches the answer is 'Not much.' They have the man-power and the expertise to just keep all the different activities running in their own strength. This, in fact, is a sign of imminent institutionalization. But when a church is small there is no one to rely on except the Lord.

There is no safety net. This can make faith and trust much more real. This is a blessed condition in which to be!

So be encouraged, small church! But having said those things we must ask the obvious question. How can we access the resources of God for his little flock?

The Holy Spirit and a small group

Any church, but especially a small church, needs the power of God. The beginning of the New Testament church saw God's great gift of power on the day of Pentecost.

The speaking in tongues at Pentecost was God's sign that the gospel was now to go to all the nations. Having restricted his activities almost exclusively to the Jewish people during the Old Testament period, now was the time for the good news to go into all the world. The foreign visitors to Jerusalem on the day of Pentecost were astonished, and exclaimed that they heard Jesus' disciples 'declaring the wonders of God in our own tongues!' (Acts 2:11). Jesus had told his disciples that they would be his witnesses 'in Jerusalem, and in all Judea and Samaria, and to the ends of the earth' (Acts 1:8).

It was to just a small group of eleven disciples that Jesus spoke in the upper room, on the night he was betrayed. He told this seemingly insignificant company about the coming of the Holy Spirit. What Jesus said to that little gathering is recorded for us in John 14–16. In those chapters Jesus repeatedly refers to the Holy Spirit as the *parakletos*. That is a word which we have had difficulty translating into English.

Sometimes we have used the word Comforter. Sometimes we have translated it as Counsellor. But neither of those words truly hits the mark. Fundamentally the word *parakletos* refers to a legal witness usually in a courtroom. So we see that in the great work of witness for Christ there are two agents. The church is called to witness. The Holy Spirit is also Christ's witness. Listen to what Jesus said to his disciples: 'When the *parakletos* comes, whom I will send to you from the Father, the Spirit of truth who goes out from the Father, he will testify about me. And you also must testify, for you have been with me from the beginning' (John 15:26–27).[1]

Christ is on trial in the courtroom of the world. The disciples then, and the church now, must speak up for Christ as his witnesses. However, the chief witness for Christ will be the Holy Spirit whom Christ sends to the church. So we are drawn to the conclusion that the church and the Holy Spirit must work hand in glove as witnesses in the world for the Lord Jesus Christ. In fact the church can only do its job as it is in step with the Spirit. It can only hold up the truth concerning the Lord Jesus as it should as it does so in the power of the Holy Spirit.

Though the original disciples, the apostles who were eyewitnesses of Jesus have now been removed to heaven, yet the Holy Spirit is still here in and among the people of the church. He too was 'with Christ from the beginning', and so is qualified to be the major witness for Christ. He was with Christ, in the unity of the Trinity, before the foundation of the world. The baby Jesus was born into this world by the wonderful workings of the Holy Spirit (Luke 1:35). The ministry of Jesus right through to his death on the cross was empowered by the Spirit (Mark 1:10; Acts 10:38; Hebrews 9:14). It was by the power of the Holy Spirit that Jesus was exalted and declared to be the Son of God by his resurrection from the dead (Romans 1:4; 1 Timothy 3:16). So the Holy Spirit is perfectly qualified for this task of witness and he is our co-worker.

- There is an *objective* side to the Spirit's witness for Christ. He is the one who led the disciples into all truth and inspired the Scriptures (John 16:13; 2 Timothy 3:16). He is also the one who attests the name of Christ by the apostolic miracles (Acts 3:16 etc.).

- There is also a *subjective* side to the Spirit's witness. He fills the disciples with assurance, joy and boldness to speak out for Jesus. One only has to remember the great change in Peter from his cowardice in the courtyard to courage before the crowds to preach Jesus Christ on the day of Pentecost to realize this. The Holy Spirit is also the one who convicts sinners' hearts of guilt and directs them to Christ the Saviour under the preaching of the gospel (John 16:7–11; Acts 2:37).

Here then we have sketched out something of the great promises concerning the Holy Spirit which the Lord Jesus gave to a small group of his followers as he had supper with them for the last time. The call comes to us, then, to glorify Christ and be his witnesses in the world in conjunction with the work of the Holy Spirit. The key resource for the church is the Spirit of God and all his work.

As well meaning as they may have been, many little churches have been discouraged by manuals about church growth. They often talk in terms of 'seeker-friendly' services, management techniques and great schemes for evangelism. These things are beyond the capabilities of most small churches. Christians who belong to small fellowships have felt as if they have been written off by such manuals. But here is the good news. Usefulness for Christ is not primarily about man-power and classy presentations. It is first and foremost to do with being filled and empowered by the Holy Spirit. All we really need to serve Christ is the Spirit of God and the Spirit's book, the Bible. In these the almighty resources of heaven are available to the smallest of groups. In that upper room, the promise of the Spirit was made to just eleven people.

Be filled with the Spirit!

The logical next step for us therefore is to contemplate the New Testament command to be filled with the Spirit (Ephesians 5:18). Even if we were a bigger church, without the Spirit of Christ we could do nothing of spiritual worth (John 15:5). Yet the magnificent encouragement to those who lack resources is that it is 'Not by might nor by power, but by my Spirit, says the LORD Almighty' (Zechariah 4:6).

How are we filled with the Holy Spirit? Whether our congregation is little or large, that is the question. How can our lives overflow with the power of the third person of the Trinity? How can each individual in our congregation know his fulness?

It is interesting that although this is such a pressing question for us the New Testament nowhere gives an answer to that precise question. Why that is we will come back to later. But although there is no concise formula given in Scripture, the Bible does give us a clear answer. I think the main thrust of Scripture teaching on this crucial matter can be summed up in terms of the four Rs. These are recognize, renounce, rededicate and rely.

Recognize

There are a number of truths which Christians ought to recognize and grasp as we think about being filled with the Spirit.

1. *If we are Christians then God has given us his Holy Spirit and the Holy Spirit dwells within us.* Paul explained to the Corinthians that their very bodies were temples of the Spirit (1 Corinthians 6:19). When we become Christians we are born of the Spirit (John 3:5). Another way of putting it is that as we turn to Christ then the Lord Jesus baptizes us with, or initiates us into, the Spirit (1 Corinthians 12:13). I am aware that others use the idea of baptism with the Spirit to speak of a 'second blessing', but I think that is a misuse of the biblical terminology. Baptism in the Spirit is what happens to us when we first become God's children and become spiritually alive. That is why the whole of Jesus' ministry could be summed up under the idea that he came to baptize with the Spirit (Mark 1:8). The Holy Spirit is within you, Christian. You may not *feel* his presence (though it is best if you do). We could not be Christians and confess that Jesus is Lord apart

from the Spirit being in us (1 Corinthians 12:3). Therefore we are to believe what the Scripture tells us. We need to recognize that we have the Spirit in our hearts. This is true of us whether we belong to a large church or a small church.

2. *We must recognize that God commands us to be filled with his Spirit.* The apostle Paul, writing under the inspiration of God tells us, 'Be filled with the Spirit' (Ephesians 5:18). As you probably know, the tense of the verb here conveys the idea of being filled and going on being filled. But the main point is that it is God's will for you to be filled with the Spirit. Sometimes when we pray to God about something, we are not sure that what we are asking is really his will. Our prayers in those situations tend to be of a more tentative nature. But there does not need to be any uncertainty about the fact that it is the Lord's will for each of us to be overflowing with the Holy Spirit. Is it God's will that Christians in small churches be filled with the Spirit? Of course it is! We have changed masters in becoming Christians. We no longer belong to the realm and rule of this world and its sin. We belong to the kingdom of God and of righteousness (Romans 6:11). It is by the Spirit that we can be empowered to begin to live God's way. Therefore the Lord wants us, each one, to be filled with his Spirit (Luke 11:13). If we fail to be filled with the Spirit it is not through any reluctance or lack on God's part.[2]

3. *We have to recognize that what blocks the work of the Holy Spirit in our lives is sin.* It is sin which causes the traffic jam that hinders the supply of the Spirit getting through. Before we can be filled with the Holy Spirit therefore we must seek to deal honestly with every known sin in our lives. That does

not mean that we must be perfect before we can be filled with the Spirit. That would defeat the Spirit's purpose and it would mean that no one would ever be filled with the Spirit. But it does mean that we humble ourselves before God. We must stop the traffic of sin and move it to the side of the motorway to clear a road for the Spirit. We must confess all our sins, and sincerely ask God's cleansing and forgiveness by the blood of Christ.

It may be extremely painful for us to face the reality of our sins. It may be that our own pride and stubbornness has been the very reason why our small church has not been blessed. Pride is often at the root of our sins. Often we would rather shift the blame to other people than confess that we have been in the wrong. Like the psalmist, we need to ask God to check out our hearts and carry out his work of conviction. 'Search me, O God, and know my heart … See if there is any offensive way in me, and lead me in the way everlasting' (Psalm 139:23–24). And when God does shine his penetrating light into our lives and strike our consciences then we must repent of our sin. That brings us to our next R.

Renounce

We may be like the rich young ruler (Matthew 19:21–22). We want what the Lord Jesus has for us, but we want to cling to our sin even more. We must not follow in the rich man's footsteps. We must turn from our sin. This has to be genuine. There is a great problem with many evangelical Christians. They know their sins. They can name them. They feel guilty about them. They confess their sins in prayer. They wish things were different. Some of them even speak to counsellors about their sins. But there is never any change. We have to say that although they have admitted their sins they have never repented of them. They are like the rich young ruler. They come with their sins to Jesus, but they will not let go of them.

To repent means to change our minds. And when we truly change our minds we change our ways. To repent means to turn away, to renounce our sins. The old Anglican service of baptism asks the candidates a question: 'Do you renounce the devil and all his works?' I like the word 'renounce', simply because we have become too comfortable with the word 'repent'. It has become part of evangelical jargon and often been watered down to mean little more than feeling a few regrets. Instead, with God's help, we are to determine to turn our backs on sin and turn to God.

- It is worth noticing the pattern of New Testament repentance for Christian believers. We find it particularly spelled out in Ephesians 4. Paul writes, 'You were taught, with regard to your former way of life, to put off the old self, which is being corrupted by its deceitful desires; to be made new in the attitude of your minds; and to put on the new self, created to be like God in true righteousness and holiness' (vv. 22–24). There is a negative and a positive. There is a putting off and a putting on. Then Paul goes on in the same chapter to make this very practical. The liar is not just to stop lying, but go on to always speak the truth (v. 25). The thief is not simply to stop stealing, he is to work so as to earn money and thus be able to give to those in need (v. 28). Those who are full of cynical, unedifying talk are to stop it and instead to speak what is encouraging and upbuilding for other people (v. 29).

• There is sometimes a fatalism which seems to afflict many Christians. They agree with all that is said about how the Lord wants them to repent and how he wants them to live, but they do not do anything about it. They seem to think that if they are to change then God must do it for them. But at the practical level we are co-workers with the Holy Spirit. He will help us, but he will not do it for us. The New Testament is clear that we have responsibility in changing our lives. Paul tells the Ephesians that *they* must put off the old and put on the new. *We* must make the effort to put off the old and put on the new. As we do this, with our faith in Christ, we will find we are not doing in our own strength, but that the Lord is aiding, strengthening and supporting us.

Sin is the great blockage to the flow of the Spirit into our lives. Therefore with God's help, we must renounce our sins if we are to be filled with the Spirit.

Once again we have already begun to touch on the next step. True repentance will lead to a new submission to the Lord and his will for our lives.

Rededicate

The way to be filled—saturated, empowered and led—by the Holy Spirit is to place the Lord Jesus Christ at the centre of our lives. The ministry of the Spirit centres around glorifying the Lord Jesus. We have seen that he comes as the *parakletos*. His great mission is to testify for Jesus Christ. If we are to be filled with the Spirit then we must have the same agenda as the Holy Spirit. That makes sense, doesn't it? If we have slipped away from this agenda then we need to rededicate our lives to this purpose.

The book of Romans speaks of this in terms of *offering* ourselves to God. '*Offer* yourselves to God, as those who have been brought from death to life; and *offer* the parts of your body to him as instruments of righteousness' (Romans 6:13). 'Therefore, I urge you, brothers, in view of God's mercy, to *offer* your bodies as living sacrifices, holy and pleasing to God—this is your spiritual act of worship' (Romans 12:1). This last verse reminds us of the Old Testament sacrifices which the worshipper presented wholly to God. He kept no part back. All was consumed on the altar. Rededication is a total surrender to the will of God.

I like the illustration that we have mentioned before of the Christian's life being like a house. You can draw a floor plan of the house with the different rooms marked. One room is labelled 'money', another 'leisure', another 'family'. Another room is labelled 'sexuality', another 'ambition', another 'time' and so on. The house of our lives has many rooms. Will the Lord be given full possession of the house? Will we let the Lord Jesus into every room to reconstruct and restore it? Will we let him set the agenda for every aspect of life? To rededicate ourselves to Christ is to say a sincere 'Yes' to the Lord.

Obviously this is a deep matter. It may involve many heart struggles. But as we sincerely seek to offer ourselves wholly to Christ, the Holy Spirit will meet us where we are and draw us on.

1. *That surrender to Christ will need to be renewed often.* There is a great temptation to somehow take back what we have laid at Jesus' feet. Vows that have been made to the Lord can be reneged on. Are you a person who has done that? If so, it is time to rededicate yourself to Christ and put your whole life at his disposal. That may mean backing out of a road you have taken in life in order to get back to the road which Christ called you to walk. There is an ongoing need to keep our life on the altar. Some Christians speak of starting each day by re-offering themselves to the Lord as they get out of bed in the morning.

2. *The Holy Spirit may test us.* He may want to see if we mean business. He may even call us to surrender something in principle which he may not call us to surrender in practice. The most striking instance of this in Scripture is found in Genesis 22. There God says to Abraham, 'Take your son, your only son, Isaac, whom you love, and go to the region of Moriah. Sacrifice him there as a burnt offering on one of the mountains I will tell you about.' Abraham, no doubt with a heavy heart, takes Isaac and obeys. On the way to the mountain Isaac asks, 'Where is the sacrifice?' not realizing that it was to be him. How heart-breaking that moment must have been for Abraham! But, of course, as Abraham proceeds and is about to sacrifice his son, God steps in. There is a voice from heaven. Abraham stops. Another sacrifice is found—the

ram caught in the thicket. Isaac is spared. And God says to Abraham, 'Now I know that you fear God, because you have not withheld from me your son.' Abraham had passed the test.

3. That surrender to the agenda of the Holy Spirit means specifically *being willing to become an active witness for the Lord Jesus Christ*. Again there may be matters of pride to be dealt with here. Perhaps we do not like the idea of being known as someone who is prepared to speak up for the Lord Jesus. Perhaps it is seen as socially embarrassing and not what nice people do. But to rededicate yourself to Christ must include this.

Rededicating our lives sincerely to Christ puts us in the position for the Spirit to fill us. We are to be slaves of Christ. In terms of today's world that very phrase might sound unacceptable. But the Lord Jesus is the best of masters. He who, in his love, gave himself entirely for us, can be trusted not to misuse us. And having said that, we have once again begun to step over into our last part of the answer to the question about how to be filled with the Holy Spirit.

Rely

This is just a synonym for faith and trust in the Lord Jesus Christ. The simple definition of faith is 'trusting the promises of God'. The Lord Jesus himself has made many wonderful promises about the giving of his Holy Spirit. 'If you then, though you are evil, know how to give good gifts to your children, how much more will your Father in heaven give the Holy Spirit to those who ask him!' (Luke 11:13). At the Feast of Tabernacles Jesus stood and said in a loud voice, 'If anyone is thirsty let him come to me and drink. Whoever believes in me, as the Scripture has said, streams of living water will flow from within him' (John 7:37–38). John, the writer, goes on to comment: 'By this he meant the Spirit, whom those who believed in him were later to receive' (John 7:39).

On the basis of such promises we are to go to the Lord in prayer and ask him to pour his Spirit into our hearts. Having recognized that it is God's will for us to be filled with the Spirit, having renounced our sins and rededicated ourselves to serve the Lord, we are to ask God to fill us with his Spirit that we might serve him in his power.

Jesus does not lie or exaggerate. We are to trust him therefore to answer such prayers. Sometimes we may be aware of God's Spirit flooding us. Sometimes we will not be. But we are to have faith that Christ is reliable and will answer us according to his grace not our deserving. Trust him. Sometimes the Spirit comes as a mighty storm (Acts 2:1–4), sometimes as a gentle dove (Mark 1:10). Rely on the Lord Jesus to furnish you with new supplies of the Holy Spirit. It is God's will that God's people and God's Spirit work hand in glove for the glory of God's Son.

If you read through the Acts of the Apostles you find that Christ's servants were filled with the Spirit on many occasions. As new opposition arises, as new opportunities come, then they are filled again. Take Peter for example. On the day of Pentecost he was one of those who was filled with the Spirit (Acts 2:4). But as he stood before the Sanhedrin, accused over the healing of the paralysed man, he was filled with the Spirit in order to answer them boldly for Christ (Acts 4:8). After this persecution had been reported, the church in Jerusalem prayed to the Lord to strengthen them to witness for Christ, and they all (presumably including Peter again) were filled with the Holy Spirit and spoke the word of God boldly (Acts 4:31). Just as Paul's command is to go on being filled with the Spirit so the filling of the Spirit is often repeated. There is one baptism in the Spirit but many fillings. As we read the Scriptures we are encouraged to trust Christ that what he did for the early church he can do for us.

If you read through the histories of people used of the Lord in the power of his Spirit you will find that their stories will always contain something of the four Rs we have mentioned above. Their circumstances, their ages, their tasks may differ markedly from one another. But you will always find they are people who have humbled themselves and renounced sin. You will always find that they are people who put their lives at God's disposal, dedicating and rededicating themselves to Christ. You will always find that they are men and women who sought the Lord and relied on him to answer their prayers to aid them with his resources.

Why is there no concise formula in Scripture for being filled with the Spirit? The answer is because the four Rs which we have pointed out are just those things of which a sincere and earnest Christian life consists, according to the New Testament. Recognizing God's gift of the Spirit to us, renouncing our sins, rededicating our lives to Christ and relying on him day by day to fill us with his strength are meant to be simply the ordinary mode of existence for every Christian.

We may well have slipped away from these things. If so, it is time to acknowledge this before the Lord and in the name of Christ come to him again along the pathway which we have spelled out. Heaven's resources are available. Our Father in heaven delights to give his Holy Spirit to those who ask.

Notes

1. *The Holy Spirit*, Sinclair B. Ferguson, IVP, 1996.
2. *The Holy Spirit*, Billy Graham, Zondervan, 1978.

11.

Jesus' letter to a small church

One of my best memories as a Dad (Ann and I have four children) is that of helping our youngsters to learn to ride a bicycle. Dad had to encourage them so, making sure they did not fall off or hurt themselves, I would hold on to the saddle and jog along behind them, stabilizing the bike while they pedalled and wobbled all over the place.

'Come on, you can do it!' I would say. There is a little car park near our house, off the road, where you can do this sort of thing. 'It's not as difficult as it seems,' I patiently urged them. And, of course, it was a great joy when they finally mastered it for themselves.

It seems to me that the Lord Jesus is a little like such a Dad with the church at Philadelphia that we read of in Revelation 3:7–13.

To the angel of the church in Philadelphia write:

These are the words of him who is holy and true, who holds the key of David. What he opens no one can shut, and what he shuts no one can open. I know your deeds. See, I have placed before you an open door that no one can shut. I know that you have little strength, yet you have kept my word and have not denied my name. I will make those who are of the synagogue of Satan, who claim to be Jews though they are not, but are liars—I will make them come and fall down at your feet and acknowledge that I have loved you. Since you have kept my command to endure patiently, I will also keep you from the hour of trial that is going to come upon the whole world to test those who live on the earth.

I am coming soon. Hold on to what you have, so that no one will take your crown. Him who overcomes I will make a pillar in the temple of my God. Never again will he leave it. I will write on him the name of my God and the name of the city of my God, the new Jerusalem, which is coming down out of heaven from my God; and I will also write on him my new name. He who has an ear, let him hear what the Spirit says to the churches.

In chapters 2 and 3 of Revelation Jesus dictates to the apostle John his seven letters to the churches. This is the sixth church to which the postman delivered Christ's letters in what is modern-day Turkey. The letter to the previous church at Sardis was a letter of almost total condemnation, because they hypocritically insisted on living on a past reputation for spiritual vitality rather than following Christ in the present. But this letter to Philadelphia is, by contrast, one of total encouragement and almost unqualified commendation.

That particularly interests me, because Philadelphia, it seems from verse 8, was a small church. 'I know that you have little strength.' Like a father with his children, the Lord Jesus Christ is encouraging this little church and urging them forward.

As we have said before, there is nothing wrong in and of itself with being a little church. If the numbers have dwindled because of sin in the church that is another thing. But as Jesus speaks to the congregation in Philadelphia there is no hint that this is the case. Rather, he commends them and spurs them on. Let us look at Jesus' word to a small church. Turning to the words of our Master provides a good way to conclude this book and we can sum up his message under three headings. Here we see Christ's authority, the church's opportunity and the promise of heaven's security.

Christ's authority (v. 7)

As with all the letters he begins by reminding them of himself.

To the angel of the church in Philadelphia write:

> These are the words of him who is holy and true, who holds the key of David. What he opens no one can shut, and what he shuts no one can open.

The natural tendency of any small and weak group is to turn inward and look at itself. But Christ first of all makes them look at him. He identifies himself as the true Messiah who controls access to the kingdom of God.

From the original language of the New Testament it is legitimate to see that Jesus speaks here of himself as 'the holy one', and 'the true one'. The Holy One, in Jewish culture, was of course a familiar title for God himself. We think of the many times the prophet Isaiah referred to the LORD as 'the Holy One of Israel' (e.g. Isaiah 1:4; 5:19; 40:25). The same phrase was also very much associated with the Messiah. As Jesus did his work of exorcism he was recognized by demons who declared him to be 'the Holy One of God' (Mark 1:24).

Similarly he introduces himself to this little church as 'the true one'. He is the genuine Christ of God, who is faithful in all his dealings. This is important. It seems from verse 9 that this little church, like us, had to contend with false religion around it. But Jesus is the genuine Messiah, the proper object of our trust, worship and devotion.

Furthermore, Jesus explains that he is the possessor of the key of David (v. 7). The key is a metaphor, indicating that Jesus has complete control and authority over the royal household, over God's kingdom. It is an expression which has been borrowed from the Old Testament. Isaiah 22:20–22 refers to Eliakim of whom God says, 'He will be a father to those who live in Jerusalem … I will place on his shoulder the key to the house of David; what he opens no one can shut, and what he shuts no one can open.' In place of Shebna the LORD would make Eliakim the steward over King Hezekiah's palace and household. He would have authority over all the servants. If you found a servant doing something you might challenge him 'What are you doing?' If he replied, 'Eliakim told me to do this,' that settled the matter. Eliakim was in control. His authority was supreme. Again, if people wanted to see King Hezekiah, and be admitted to his presence, then first they had to get permission from Eliakim.

It is not difficult to see how this prefigures the Lord Jesus in his role as Messiah. He has the key. He is the only one who can admit people into fellowship with God. 'I am the way and the truth and the life,' said Jesus. 'No one comes to the Father except through me' (John 14:6; see also John 10:9). He has undisputed authority to admit or exclude from the New Jerusalem. Christ has absolute power to control entrance to, and service within, the heavenly kingdom. This is how the Lord Jesus introduces himself to the little flock at Philadelphia. He emphasizes his authority.

As chief steward

It may be that these believers in Philadelphia were Jewish and had been excluded, excommunicated from the local synagogue (v. 9), because of their faith in the Lord Jesus Christ. But Christ is reminding them that it is not what earthly priests and religious leaders think of them that matters. All power in heaven and on earth has been given to him! What do others think of us? Other Christians, other churches? Obviously we should do our utmost to live in harmony with all true churches. But if bigger churches despise you, do not worry. It is what Jesus, the chief steward over God's kingdom, thinks of us that really matters.

As head of the church

However, this unparalleled position of Jesus also brings every church a challenge. This applies to churches both big and small. If there was one thing which grated with me when I began as a pastor it came whenever I heard people, even well-meaning people, referring to the congregation as 'my church'. In fact I did not even like it when people in our own congregation talked about 'our church'. The great glory of the church is that it is the Lord's church. Even the smallest group of the Lord's people, who with a biblical discipline meet regularly together to encourage one another and evangelize the district, belong to the Lord. The church is his property. He is the head. He is the owner. Not the pastor. Not the elders. Not even the people themselves. We are not our own. We have been bought at the great price of Christ's blood.

Of course, there is a right way to speak about 'our church'. If that phrase refers to the fact that we belong to it, that we love the fellowship of which we are members, that this local church is our particular sphere of service, then that is fine. But somehow that phrase 'our church' can easily carry the idea not simply that we belong to the church but rather that the church belongs to us. When we slip, even unconsciously, into thinking like that we are very wrong. The problem is that in independent churches with a congregational basis of church government (with which my experience makes me most familiar) this kind of mentality can hold sway. The members support the church financially. They come to the church meetings. They discuss and perhaps take votes on issues. They make decisions. Warmth and unity among the members and fellow feeling for one another is good. But even these good things can sometimes fuel the vision of the church as our 'religious club'. Such a cosy attitude has been a deadly disease in many fellowships. The church is not our church. It is the Lord's church.

Now with that assurance of his transcendent authority over the church very much at the forefront of their minds, the Lord Jesus next reminds the church in Philadelphia of what he has set before them.

Their opportunity (vv. 8–10)

Look at verse 8:

> I know your deeds. See, I have placed before you an open door that no one can shut. I know that you have little strength, yet you have kept my word and have not denied my name.

In Scripture, there is an open door of salvation. The Lord Jesus speaks of himself as the door into the fold of God's sheep (John 10:9). To be one of Christ's flock is to be saved. The open door speaks of a free invitation to all to come and be saved. All may find the blessing of sins forgiven, peace with God and eternal life, by God's grace.

But here, the Lord Jesus is speaking to people who are already saved. They have kept Christ's word and not denied his name. They are faithful followers of the Lord Jesus. They are God's people. So here, the open door is not one of salvation, but rather an open door of service. The picture of the open door is often used in the New Testament as a picture of opportunity to serve. It is used particularly as an opportunity for evangelism.

Consider some of the occasions on which the apostle Paul used this picture. He explains to the church in Corinth that he intends to stay on in Ephesus for a while because 'a great door for effective work has opened to me' (1 Corinthians 16:9). Again, when he writes to Corinth a second time he describes how when he went to Troas to preach the gospel of Christ he found that 'the Lord had opened a door for me' (2 Corinthians 2:12). When he writes from prison to the church in Colosse he encourages them to pray 'that God may open a door for our message, so that we may proclaim the mystery of Christ, for which I am in chains' (Colossians 4:3).

It seems then that for the little church in Philadelphia a door of service had been opened and the Lord Jesus was saying 'Go on. You can do it. Go through that door.' Like a Dad with his children, he was encouraging them saying, 'It's not as difficult as it looks. I've opened the door for you.'

If you are a member of a small congregation, perhaps it is this particular message with which the Lord would challenge you as you read this book. I do not know your circumstances at all. Are there people reading this with whom the Lord has been dealing? Perhaps you are a leader of a fellowship. Perhaps you know there is some kind of opportunity which has opened up. Are you deliberating? What is the Lord saying through this book? Is he saying, 'Go on, even though you are few in number, for my kingdom'?

The opportunity for service was there before the church at

Philadelphia. But somehow they were not moving forward. That was why the Lord Jesus sent the letter to encourage them. What was making them hesitate? What was holding them back? I think, from verses 8–10, we can discern three reasons. And these three reasons are obstacles which often hold back little churches. What were these three things which made them hesitate? I believe it was their weakness, their self-doubt and their fear.

Their weakness (v. 8)

> I know that you have little strength, yet you have kept my word and have not denied my name.

They had little strength. They were such a small fellowship. So they asked themselves, 'Do we really have the resources to serve the Lord? Do we really have the ability to evangelize? Can we honestly do anything to care for people in the vicinity? Are we able to take up this opportunity?' They were lacking in manpower. That may be true of you. But Jesus still urges the church at Philadelphia forward. Christ has reminded them that he has all authority. He is bidding them to take up the opportunity, and surely he will provide for them out of his limitless power. And as we said at the start of this book, very often small churches are in a much better position to ensure that all the glory goes to Christ. It took just two men, Jonathan and his armour-bearer, to scale the cliff, destroy twenty of the enemy and put the whole Philistine army in a panic (1 Samuel 14:1–15). The result was that everyone knew that the LORD had rescued Israel that day (1 Samuel 14:23). And do you remember what Jonathan said to his armour-bearer that day? 'Nothing can hinder the LORD from saving, whether by many or by few' (1 Samuel 14:6). God loves to use small numbers. So 'Go on', says the Lord Jesus, 'I have all authority and I am with you.' The main thing is that the church had been faithful to Jesus and his gospel (v. 8). Now he will be faithful to them. So, despite your weakness, 'Go on,' says Christ.

Their self-doubt

It seems to me that this little group of believers was despised in their locality. This comes across especially from verse 9. They had been despised by those of the synagogue of Satan. (This could be any religious group but probably represents Jewish opposition, see Revelation 2:9.) In particular it seems that this hatred went along with the slur 'God does not love you.' 'Look how weak you are!' they said. 'That shows that you know nothing of the blessing of God.' And inevitably when such things are said, it knocks a congregation's confidence. It does Satan's work of sowing self-doubt. The little church finds itself thinking, 'There's something wrong with us. We are no good.' It puts a dark cloud over them. How many little churches suffer under that kind of reputation, simply because they are few in number? It was because of the slur 'God does not love you' that the Lord Jesus Christ says, 'I will make those who are of the synagogue of Satan, who claim to be Jews though they are not, but are liars—I will make them come and fall down at your feet and acknowledge that I have loved you' (v. 9). No, do not be taken in by Satan's hurtful words. Are you seeking to honestly love and obey Christ? Then, little church, Jesus loves you.

Do not doubt it. He is not like the world, only enamoured with the big and glossy. He is the Saviour who noticed and rejoiced in the widow's mite (Luke 21:1–4).

Their fear

When we are weak, we are more prone to fear. Throughout the book of Revelation the storm clouds are gathering. They are thunder clouds of opposition. In Revelation we meet the Beast who represents government-sponsored persecution. We also meet the false prophet who opposes the gospel through false religion and lying ideologies. Besides these two grim customers, we meet the great prostitute of Babylon, who would seduce the church into worldly ways and so destroy it. All these come at the church at various times to frighten and terrorize us. Our reaction, especially as we feel weak, is to say to ourselves, 'It's best to keep quiet. It is best not to draw attention to ourselves.' As we face the scorn of secular society or downright threats of persecution and violence from fanatical groups, some people counsel the church to stop evangelizing, to stop serving the Lord. But Jesus encourages the small congregation at Philadelphia to reject such counsel. 'Go on,' he urges. He promises in verse 10: 'Since you have kept my command to endure patiently, I will also keep you from the hour of trial that is going to come upon the whole world to test those who live on the earth.'

Perhaps it is not fear of persecution which haunts many small churches. Perhaps it is fear of failure in service, anxiety about trying something and falling flat on our faces. The ego of a little church can feel very vulnerable to any kind of embarrassment. But what we learn from Scripture is that it is better to have tried and failed (will the Lord ultimately allow that?) for Christ than not to have tried at all. Remember the parable of talents (Matthew 25:24–26). The returning Lord was not pleased with the servant who simply buried what he had been given. Christ is promising that if we serve him, he will protect us and keep us until our work is done, and then he will take us home. The testing that comes upon the world will sweep many into a lost eternity (v. 10). They will be found wanting. But not those who sincerely seek to obey Christ.

So having pointed them first to himself, the Lord Jesus has shown the small church the open door of opportunity he has set before them and has answered their hesitations. 'Go on,' he is saying.

In this book I have tried to set out how small churches can still work for the Lord. We have thought about quality presence in the community. We have seen the need for quality welcome and quality teaching within the church. We have explored the possibilities available through quality hospitality outside the confines of the church building. We have been encouraged to think about what can be achieved through quality prayer. Here are open doors for us all.

Having issued such a challenge, Jesus now goes on to explain the reward that awaits those who obediently go through the open door of service.

Heaven's security (vv. 11–12)

Hold on to what you have, so that no one will take your crown. Him who overcomes I will make a pillar in the temple of my God. Never again will he leave it. I will write on him the name of my God and the name of the city of my God, the new Jerusalem, which is coming down out of heaven from my God; and I will also write on him my new name.

Here is the promise of the Lord Jesus. There are three aspects here and these are reward, service and ownership.

Reward

The little church battling away for Christ can be tempted to give up and throw in the towel. But they should keep on striving: 'Hold on to what you have, so that no one will take your crown.' A crown awaits in heaven for all those who love the Lord and keep going in their service for him (2 Timothy 4:8). The going is hard. But now is not the time to give up. Do not let anyone or anything rob you of that crown in heaven. Those who have been belittled, troubled and sneered at on earth in the cause of Christ will be applauded in heaven. They will be able to wear their crown with a Christian pride. 'Since, little church, you have been despised on earth for my name,' the Lord is telling them, 'do not sell yourselves short by forfeiting your heavenly crown.' 'Go on,' and 'Keep going on,' are the watchwords of true Christianity.

Service

Serving Christ thrills the Christian's soul. To be useful to the glorious Lord of the whole universe is the highest privilege of sinful creatures like ourselves. 'That *God* should use me!' we say to ourselves in amazement, 'I can scarcely believe it!' But at the same time service can be risky, or at least seem so. 'Him who overcomes I will make a pillar in the temple of my God. Never again will he leave it.' There are many temptations, battles, journeys and insecurities along the way of serving Christ. But the picture of the future of the Christian becoming a pillar in God's temple seems to combine the blessing of service while at the same time eliminating the risk. The pillar in God's temple is of enormous use. It holds up the roof. It is essential.

It is so easy for people in small churches to see themselves and their service as unimportant and dispensable. But here, the Lord Jesus is promising them a position of indispensable service in his kingdom. How thrilling that is to those who love to serve Christ! Yet at the same time, a pillar in God's temple is never moved. It never has to venture out. It is continually basking in the presence of the Lord. It is safe and secure. So the idea of the pillar combines the best of both worlds.

Recently a group of us had an experience that gave us a small taste of this. We had to go out to Kenya (as we have done before) to take a Christian conference far from the capital. Before we went, there had been bad news of terrorist attacks attempted against aeroplanes. There had also been some local violence following a change of government. 'Should we go?' we asked ourselves. After all, our wives were meant to be coming along too.

To cut a long story short, the Lord gave us clear guidance that despite the possible troubles we should go. We did and God blessed remarkably. But the strange thing was that we felt completely safe the whole time as people were praying for us. In fact it was dangerous. There was at least one shooting and one theft of cattle which took place nearby while we were there. But we just knew God with us; and so we felt totally at home. We experienced a taste of this lovely combination of being both useful to the Lord while at the same time totally secure. 'Well,' say our verses here, 'that's a little taste of heaven.' It points to the fact that both the best and the safest place to be in the world is right in the middle of the Lord's will. So go on, little church.

Ownership

The Lord Jesus then concludes:

> I will write on him the name of my God and the name of the city of my God, the new Jerusalem, which is coming down out of heaven from my God; and I will also write on him my new name.

When we write our name on something we show it belongs to us. From the day we wrote our name on our exercise books at school to the day we write a security code on our car, we are proclaiming, 'This belongs to me!' The Lord Jesus promises the little church at Philadelphia that as they go on to take the opportunity of service he has set before them, they will find various names inscribed upon themselves. They will bear God's name, showing they belong to him. They will find the name of God's city, new Jerusalem, showing that they are citizens of that place, never to be excluded. They will find that Jesus will be unashamed to own them. The new name of Jesus will be inscribed upon them and their lives. Not the name simply of Jesus, the despised carpenter of Nazareth, but that new name of Jesus Christ the risen and victorious Lord of all.

So many little flocks are small independent fellowships. 'Who are you?' people ask. Other small churches can find themselves almost disowned by their own denominations. At conferences they are not given the prominence or attention given to big thriving churches. But as they faithfully serve Christ, he will own them. In heaven he will show in the most undisputed way that those who have faithfully served him in little congregations belong to him.

Here then are wonderful promises to encourage those who labour for the Lord in small fellowships. Little church, you are not insignificant. Jesus says, 'I know your deeds.' They do not go unnoticed by the Lord. The devil tells you that your work for Christ means nothing. But that is a lie. The Master has you lovingly in his eye. And he would say, 'Go on.'

There are things that need changing in the church, no doubt. Perhaps in reading this manifesto for small churches you have gained a new vision of the way forward. Perhaps you can now see the future and what needs to be done with more clarity. The final thought from Christ's word to the small church at Philadelphia is the most important. Realize the Lord Jesus did not address this letter just to the pastor, or even to just the elders, deacons, church committee or whatever. Rather, he addressed it to the whole church. That leaves us all, whoever we are, with a response to make to Christ's challenge and word of encouragement. The spiritual needs of our land are immense. In every city and town and village there are people who desperately need the love of God. The door is open. The choice is before you. What are you going to do?

'He who has an ear, let him hear what the Spirit says to the churches.'

Appendix

Notes on preparing a sermon

It may be that you are part of a very small church which is in need of Bible ministry and though you have had no formal training, it falls to you to do your best to preach and teach the Bible to the church. The whole matter of handling the Word of God helpfully and opening it up so that others are encouraged in their faith is a big subject. However, the following notes may give you at least a few pointers to help you in this great and necessary task.

Basic convictions

- We need to be called by God to the work (1 Timothy 3:1; Acts 13:1–3).

- Our calling is to preach the Word (2 Timothy 4:2; Titus 1:9; Mark 16:15). The Word of God is more fundamental than the visual image (Hebrews 11:3) and by it comes life (James 1:18; 1 Peter 1:23).

- We are not called to be original, we are called to exalt God and edify people.

Ten fundamental ingredients

1. Prayerful preparation

Anything which is of spiritual worth is born in prayer. Our messages do not merely have to be academically accurate, but must also have the touch of heaven on them (Colossians 4:3–4).

2. Arresting introduction

In a busy world, people's minds are filled with all kinds of things. You must grab their attention. Start where they are and lead them to God. Note Jesus' arresting introductions, e.g. Matthew 5:3; Luke 10:30; note Nathan, 2 Samuel 12.

3. Exegetical accuracy

We must convey the truth which the text is meant to convey—not reading our ideas into it. The four crucial areas are: grammar—context—genre—redemptive history. We should seek to legitimately find Christ in all the Scriptures (Luke 24:27; John 5:39; 2 Timothy 3:15).

4. Doctrinal substance

The key to personal transformation is the mind (Romans 12:2). Therefore our explanation of Scripture must convey, not just stories, but definite Bible truths—the counsel of God (Acts 20:27), which gives discernment.

5. Clear structure

Generally people can grasp a message and retain it better if they can see a clear structure behind what is being said. Can you see the structure in Peter's sermon in Acts 2?

6. Vivid illustration

Illustrations act like windows into truth. They can grab the imagination and enable people to see the potential of the truth. They underline the truth for people and help them to grasp it. This is also the place (occasionally and humbly) for the preacher's personal experience. Personal experience gives evidence that God's truth works in practice.

7. Reasoned argument

Calvin argues that rationality is a great part of God's image in us. Reasonable people need a reasonable faith. We should bring the force of logic into our preaching—without becoming convoluted (Acts 6:9–10; 9:22).

8. Spiritual urgency

We are not academic teachers, we are preachers. Ultimately we have a life-or-death message to share with people. We need fire in us as well as light! We need to be filled with the Spirit.

9. Pointed application

Our hearers need to know what they must do practically in the light of the message. Note that different people require different applications (1 Thessalonians 5:14; 2 Timothy 3:16–17).

10. Decisive conclusion

Our messages must not peter out. Generally speaking sermons must travel, starting where the people are, to a clear, practical and decisive conclusion. Note Matthew 7:24–27; Acts 2:36, 38.

General method

So, in coming to speak on a passage of Scripture, our first prayerful task is to determine the main truth (or truths) which the passage is meant to convey (points 3 and 4).

Having done this we should work on creating a clear and if possible logical structure (points 5 and 7) which conveys the truth, and pray for that truth to grip our own hearts (point 8). ('What comes from the heart, goes to the heart' George Whitefield.)

As the truth has impacted us we should then be in a position to see to what conclusion (point 10) we want to bring the people. If we can encapsulate that conclusion in a brief, punchy sentence, so much the better. (Sometimes it is good to use that punch-line a number of times in the sermon.)

We are then in a position to go back to our structure and work on the different subsections. Within each subsection we need to:

1. State the truth (point 4)   (mind)

2. Illustrate the truth (point 6)   (imagination/emotions)

3. Apply the truth (point 9)   (will)

but keep sight of the ultimate conclusion (point 10)—see Philippians 2:5–16 as an example of the method of 'state, illustrate, apply'.

Now it is time to think about the introduction (point 2). How can you get hold of people's attention in order to lead them into the truth?

Scripture Index